# QUEEN OF JACKS
## Stellasue Lee

I first came across Stellasue Lee's poems in 1995 and was impressed by their power.

Then, in 2010, I wrote a blurb for her book *Firecracker RED*, and found that power had strengthened.

And now, in the year 2019, upon reading *The Queen of Jacks,* I find that power has grown *stronger still.*

Each poem in the six sections of *The Queen of Jacks* has its own integrity, but in aggregate, almost like a novel, and without a spot of sensationalism, they tell the story of a poet's life, from a harsh childhood with absentee parents to ultimate success, not only as a poet, but also as a tennis player and teacher.

I was captured by the first poem in the collection and read through to the end.

John Bennett, author and editor

# QUEEN OF JACKS

## Stellasue Lee

BOMBSHELTER PRESS
Los Angeles 2019

Cover art by Eric L. Hansen
Layout and design by Baz Here
ISBN: 978-0-941017-32-9

BOMBSHELTER PRESS
www.bombshelterpress.com
6684 Colgate Ave.
Los Angeles, CA 90048

Printed in the United States of America

# ACKNOWLEDGEMENTS

I wish to thank the following literary journals where these poems first appeared:

*After Shocks: The Poetry of Recovery for Life-Shattering Events*, "Change of Season," and "Out of Nowhere"

*Blood Pudding*, "Cheers," "Monterey," and "Sighted"

*Cultural Weekly*: "Purity"

*Filtered through Time*: "How to Hold Your Arms When You're in Love," and "My Alexandria"

*Free&D*: "Beyond the Paddock, Stable, Ring," "South on I-65, Take the Lewisburg Pike Turnoff," "Standing in Front of Marilyn Monroe's Crypt, Westwood, California," "Valley Through the Hill," and "While Setting the Table"

*MiPOesias*: "Dutch Masters"

*News From Inside*: "One Night in the Life of a Poet," and "Rituals

*Raising The Roof*, Habitat for Humanity: "Into That Black Night"

*So Luminous the Wildflowers*: "Without Looking Back"

*Sounding Off*, Women Writers West: "Morning on the Sound"

*Voices From the Valley*: "Alone with Children," "Last Dance," "Pictures"

*We Used To Be Wives*: "My Name is Stellasue," and "Report"

*Women and Death*: "Last Dance"

*American Journal of Poetry*: "Beauty" and "Reading the Stars"

*Animus,* : "How to Hold Your Arms When You're in Love"

*Cedar Hill Review*: "Listen, Please Listen"

*Connecticut Review*: "Dusting," "Empty Drawers," "Grief: a Great Sadness, Especially as a Result of a Death...," "Life Cycle," "Stargaze," and "To the Living"

*Cortland Review*: "Ah, Men," and "James Bond Beach"

*Carnegie Writers' Group*: "Connecting the Dots"

*Herman Literary Review*: "Fishing," and "Windows"

*Inertia Magazine*: "Witness"

*Inky Blue*: "Distortion" and "Expedition"

*Margie*: "A Documentary on Morning"

*Ol' Chanty-Chanticleer Magazine*: "A Continuous Spectrum of Color," "After a 500-Year Flood," "Children Are Not Supposed To Die Before Their Parents," "Drinking from the Many Waters of Hades," "Grief," "Old Age," "Ode to Broken Bones," "Reading the Stars," "Resume," and "Theory of Flux"

*On Target*: "At Twenty-two," "Morning," and "North on 101"

*ONTHEBUS*: "A Wall Through Woods on Hood Canal," "Crows," "Gifts for the Moon," "Old Woman," and "The Earthquake," "Magic," "September Can Be the Very Best Month," "After a Thousand Tragedies," "What I've Never Told Anyone," "Beauty," and "A Prediction of Armageddon

*Psaltery & Lyre*: "Admission"

*Paterson Literary Review*: "James Bond Beach," " Loose Limbed and Weeping," and "This Day"

*Pearl*: "Children, in Praise Of..." and "Ask Me"

*Poetrybay*" "Change of Season"

*Quercus Review*: "My Alexandria"

*Red Brick Review*: "I told Him My Name Was Amelia."

*Sheila-Na-Gig*: "Report" and "Do It"

*Spillway*: "My Name Is Stellasue" and "Fishing"

*Sulphur River Literary Review*: "Gifts for the Moon"

*Terminus*: "About Attachments"

*The American Journal of Poetry*: "Between Life and Loss" and "Reading the Stars"

*The Más Tequila Review*: "After the War," "Darkly I Enter the Ring," "Dutch Masters," "Flying at Night Without a Moon," "Her Honey-Bunch, Gum-Drop, Sweetie-Pie Is Gone," "Lost as a Hunter Home From the Hill" and "While Setting the Table"

*Voices*: "North, on 101," "Red Corvette," "The Last Dance," "The Queen of Jacks" and "This Life"

*Vol. No.*: "No Way Has Yet Been Invented To Say Goodbye" and "Things My Father Said"

I also wish to thank the following people: Eric L Hansen for his unwavering support, Linda Parsons for her proofing skills and friendship, and to Jack Grapes, Bambi Here and Baz Here for their belief in my work.

## POETRY BOOKS BY STELLASUE LEE

*Our Father*

*firecracker RED*

*Crossing the Double Yellow Line*

*13 Los Angeles Poets*

*Over to You*

*After I Fall*

## CHAPBOOKS BY STELLASUE LEE

*Sparrow's Egg Lady's Slipper*

*A Strange Wind That Blows*

*Moon of Yellow-jacketed Faithfulness*

*Winter Winds Blow Cold*

*Moon Child*

*Heart Sound*

*Spring '90*

*You're Only as Good as Your Last Move*

*For Eric,*
*Not long after we married, a psychic told me marrying you had been the best*
*decision of my life to date. It turns out he was correct. This is for you.*

# ONE

*KNUCKLEBONES INTACT*

# TWO

*LIKE A PALETTE OF RAIN CLOUDS,*
*EYES THE COLOR OF YOUNG RICE*

# THREE

## *THE SCARCE SIDE OF MERCY*

# FOUR

*I'M TELLING YOU, I WAS READY FOR ANYTHING*

# FIVE

## *DARK LEDGE OF NIGHT*

# SIX

*ABOVE GROUND*

# ONE
## KNUCKLEBONES INTACT

*"Courage doesn't always roar. Sometimes courage is the quiet voice at the end of the day, saying, "I will try again tomorrow."*

–Mary Anne Radmacher

# THE QUEEN OF JACKS

Jacks was my game—
early morning sitting on cold concrete
picking up splits with the sweep of my hand.
I knew where to toss the ball and just how high,
I was the *Queen of Jacks.*

The boys would be around the corner
pitching pennies, or shooting marbles,
(all in the thumbs)
bragging over some old cat's eye,
or puree; boulders were the big ones.

Me, I was the *Queen of Jacks,*
a title that never followed me anywhere.
I wore an anklet with my name engraved
just to identify myself.
A string-bean kid with limp colorless hair,

taking my lunch money across the street
to the soda fountain, climbing up on a swivel stool
and asking for *The Usual,*
which meant apple pie a la mode.
I can tell you,

there were plenty of days I gagged on that good thing,
It could have been liver and I would have eaten it
just so the next day I could walk in and say, *The Usual,*
and the guy behind the counter would know
the *Queen of Jacks* was there for lunch.

# WHAT I'VE NEVER TOLD ANYONE

The old woman down the block yelled at us every time my brother and I stepped one foot off the sidewalk. Her lawn was emerald, the most perfect grass I had ever seen. Leaving for school one morning, I poured a fistful of salt into my hand, walked down the block and tossed it on her lawn. For weeks, I had to watch it die, watch the old woman pray over each scrawny root that reached deep into tainted soil. I saw it spread, turn everything in its path brown. I would see her standing over it, looking deep between delicate leaves for an answer to the mystery. I couldn't look at that battleground of leaf and earth. It was a year before we moved, and it still hadn't recovered.

The kids in school called me Silly Sue. A boy took my lunch money every day, so I went to work in the cafeteria and got lunch free. Mother thought I did it to help out, and I let her think so, but I didn't.

Elwood Simpson kissed me behind the blackboard at school. Somehow, Mother found out. Father spanked me for lying and I peed all over him. He vomited in the toilet and screamed at my mother for telling him to hit me.

Two years later, Mother packed his things and kicked him out. Brother asked why, she told him that our father got on her nerves. My brother said that I was getting on *his* nerves too.

We were so poor, only one of us got a Christmas gift. One year my brother got a gift, the next, I got something.

Our mother had a bad stomach. She couldn't eat anything but canned baby food. The owner of a mom & pop store gave her a case of baby food with the labels soaked off. I punched a tiny whole in the bottom of a few to see if I liked them. I didn't, and put them back in the cupboard.

My fourth-grade teacher was Martha Kramer, Jack Kramer's sister. She took me to a ballet, symphony, and *Madama Butterfly*. I got my first library card and nothing was ever the same.

## TILL THOU AT LENGTH ART FREE, LEAVING THINE OUTGROWN SHELL BY LIFE'S UNRESTING SEA!
–Oliver Wendell Holmes

It's April, my father's birth month. Things had been
bad for him, then the war. Of course he went—
duty, country. Hell, his brother was living

in Hawaii when bombs rained on Pearl Harbor.
Dad was accustomed to a shattered existence.
Once home, life still didn't go well.

He lost an eye—thanks to a doctor who didn't
use sterilized instruments to remove a hunk of steel,
and Dad, not wearing goggles while welding.

So, he read, oh, he read just about everything.
Even blind in one eye, he kept on reading.
And he believed anything was possible

in books, you know—he had himself
convinced, if he read enough,
any minute he would find a happy ending.

## STANDING UPRIGHT

The mortuary left a note taped to the door
announcing my mother's death. They're trained,
I suppose, in the delicate art of disclosure.
A card, the kind I use to send recipes to friends.
On the day she died,
the same date my father died
three years earlier, I think,
gray rain—some master bright-light plan
to crack me apart. I stand, land upright
but don't see any humor unfolding.

No strip-mined fly-in-the-face set-up,
no put-down event
is going to take me out.
Let this be understood,
I will survive, and they will know
whoever they are.
I refused to see my mother in death.

I am twenty-six and childless,
my own mortality is at stake.
No child comes forth, no kin of mine,
no blood of my blood
courses through young, strong veins,
no child to suckle-sweet at my breast.

That dream continues for twenty-four years.
Each new month I survive mounds of blood clots,
endless rivers of red, until it is clear, even to me,
one of us has to die, the dream,
or me? I think, me, or the dream?

I am six and take care of my dolls.
They need to be dressed and fed.
Grownups ask, What do you want to be when you grow up?
I say, *A mother, with lots of children.*
They wring their hands at such single-mindlessness,
such tunnel vision.

I can tell you, not once, I swear not once,
did I conceive of a life without children.
Always, there was to be one at the hem of my dress,
one at my breast.
Now this child's dream is dead.
The mother and the father, dead.
What of the dead?
They stare with sightless eyes,
stone-cold hands rest over empty, beatless chests,
hands that wring no more.

Let this be understood:
I continue:
dreamless,
bloodless,
childless,
I stand,
knucklebones intact.

# DARKLY I ENTER THE RING

My father left school when he was fourteen and joined the Navy—
a fellow could do that back then, lie about his age, doctor-up
his birth certificate, or present a letter from his mom,

even if he had to doctor-up that too. He came out a man, shaving,
all spiffed up, wearing better duds than he'd ever been given
as a boy. So, what seemed natural to him was to reenlist,

but this time, man that he was, he went into the Marine Corps,
traded one uniform for another to walk around in,
cocksure of himself. He got into boxing. Every chance he'd get,

into the ring he went. He knew the four corners better
than most men know their own back door, the one they enter
and leave by every day. It was nothing to him,

a broken nose, ten stitches, twenty stitches above an eye,
shattered cheekbone,  a few thousand split lips—
it was all better than being a sweet boy with sun-bleached hair.

I got into the ring myself once, *his* baby girl, lifted the top rope
as he would have done, paced corner to corner, jabbed into the air
just to feel power in my back, my arms. I even tossed myself

against the ropes to feel that sensation of being thrown back
into the game. I got down on hands and knees, experienced
canvas in my face. I didn't feel what I think my dad must have felt,

even though it was all there for me. I felt nothing,
except the dark presence of his sheer stubbornness in youth.

## TRANSCENDING SELF

A window is open this morning,
air—cool as whipped butter,
thick in texture, moist as tears.

The sprinklers went off at 4 AM
and the ground, wet and rich,
is dark, trembling with life. A robin

searches carefully, and with sudden
movement, pulls a long worm
from the mire. I shouldn't say this,

I don't want to go back in time,
but a brown dress I made
and wore on Career Day

of my senior year in high school
returns to mind. Every detail,
the soft lining of silk, pencil-thin

skirt, my intention to make
a life in aerospace. Somewhere
there still exists a picture

documenting this entire event.
For crying out loud, I can't imagine
what I was thinking back then,

maybe that *Glass Ceiling* women
my age talked about, life working in
a factory, living paycheck to paycheck,

poetry such a void in my soul,
I could not discern then what it meant
to simply accept life's ordinary details.

# FUZZY THINKING

When I was twelve, my mother stopped smoking.
It was sensible, what with the Surgeon General's

warning and all. She did what millions did,
quit, and packed on twenty extra pounds.

Weight gain was the difficult part, she had said,
and of course, I being twelve, knew everything,

so I vowed never to gain an ounce. Smoking was
out of the question. Forty-five years later,

I met a man I thought I wanted to impress.
I had learned nothing about good choices in men.

He offered me a cigarette and I demurely
declined. I may have even batted my eyelashes.

*You don't smoke? No, I've never smoked. Why*, he asked,
and because I'm an honest person, one not always

able to access my own thinking process, I replied
most unreasonably, *Because I don't want to put on weight.*

That pretty much ended the evening. I mean, what bad
boy could look into eyes of clear water and not see

that further dates are pointless. But I wondered
what other decisions I had made as a child, influenced

my adult life so that I would respond with the force
of a rushing stream, the kind that wears away rock.

## BLEMISH

I stare into the many facets of a diamond
I wear on the third finger of my left hand.
My mother's ring. This stone so hard, it withstood
her life and death, all her disassembly: psoriasis,
high blood pressure, drunkenness, divorce, nights
driving home after the swing shift. She had it on
when she pulled her car to the side of a quiet highway
and went to sleep forever.

The surface of this brilliant stone is smooth, shape-shifting
all the colors of my world around its edges.
I let my vision drift and blur inside, hoping for
a discovery, answers somehow revealed,
our future foretold, the past reconciled.
I know the stone is strong, just one tiny flaw
that floats within its universe, like the two parts
of myself. How silent our thoughts can seem, each of us
flawed and strong, fragmented and brilliant.

## FLAT

on my back, I look up to identify
shapes that appear out of a concrete ceiling—

a small child holds out her hands,
a puppy with black eyes and a slight

imperfection for its nose. There are
many others to keep me company

as light plays from the cars six stories
below—an old woman, her mouth

round with surprise, a boat,
afloat in ripples made by the pour.

Once, when I was feverish, I saw the
most amazing thing. It was early morning,

I think, and the ceiling became liquid—
waves lapping at walls, but later,

the concrete seemed to have set again
and I didn't worry enough to sort it out.

That night there were church bells.
I slept in uneven shadows, woke hungry.

# ODE TO BROKEN BONES

The clavicle, fractured in two places—left side of body.
Blunt trauma falling off a bicycle in *Mazatlán*
off the coast of Mexico.

Compound fracture of the right foot—twenty-six bones
found there, four have been on the receiving end of trauma
while cleaning the house. O Lord, is there a lesson here?

Six ribs of the thoracic cage—broken three times.
Once in a car driven by a murderous cab driver,
again, by a wave that had the strength of Hercules,
a third time by a man who meant no harm when his
arm swung out at the exact moment I rose from a chair.

Navicular bone, broken wrist—with a retrograde blood
supply that feeds the bone and bone cells—snapped
when right hand made contact with the floor to break a fall.

O Lord, please, show mercy on this oft-mended soul.

# GAME, SET, MATCH

I've played tennis, played seven, maybe eight hours
a day, sometimes twice on Sundays. I know how
a ball hits soft on a lawn-green court in England.

I've come off a clay court in Spain with red dust covering my fair skin,
turning my ash hair strawberry blond.

I've played singles, doubles, and round-robins.
I've played Wimbledon, bend-your-knees,
hit-the-ball-hard tennis.

I've socked it to them on the West Coast, East Coast,
Hawaii, Tahiti, Fiji, Austria, France, Belgium
and all the places in between.

Driving west on Roscoe Boulevard, a car runs the light,
broadsides me. I am pinned in the wreckage,
on display, under glass.

Doctors in an ER say I'll never walk again. They shake
their heads, mumble something that sounds like
years of recovery. I say I'm going home, home to heal.

In my mind, I play tennis all day, backhand, forehand,
overhead smash. I hit buckets of imaginary balls,
work though days of pain, nights of agony

on my game, my game. Three months later I'm back
on a court, lacing up run-over shoes, fastening a short,
white skirt. I run, bend my knees, hit the ball          hard.

## ABSCESS

A bald dentist, all forehead and white teeth,
uses an explorer to point out the darkened bulb

at the apex of my upper right first molar in an X-ray.
*Have you suffered a blow to the right side of your face?*

I remember that second between calm and order,
chaos and fracture, Alice down the rabbit hole,

strange landscape and odd characters, red screaming
sirens, white hospital masks and the smell of blood.

## SKILLED NURSING, ROOM 104 A

Quiet, except for the long stream of breath
that sounds now and again from the other side
of a curtained-off area. She is now small,

so small, perhaps as much as a third of what
had been her body weight. I awaken to rain.
Not the soft rain of summer, but fierce,

so that hydrangeas and chrysanthemums
droop, rose petals fall in a heap
about their roots. For two days, she has been

reaching into the air above her. I'd like to think
reaching for new life, waiting to walk out
of her body, waiting to join her husband.

*Daddy,* she calls for him, *Daddy, help me!*
*Daddy*…and I lie in this semiprivate room,
the same bed he died in ten months before,

and count the beaten chrysanthemums
trusting Daddy hears her, Daddy will come
for his wife of sixty-seven years.

# REINVENTION OF OUR NIGHTS

We no longer sit around eating fresh fruit or drinking wine.
My husband and I head off for the gym.

We know exercise is best done in the morning, but we're
retired, working harder, harder than ever before.

I'm spinning again, spin to my own music. I don't bother to turn
any overhead lights on. I spin in a semi-darkened room

with only shimmering floor lights from the gymnasium
shining into the curved bowl of a spin studio.

I sing along with my iPod, sing as I spin, sing as if in a church
choir, a familiar hymn that fills my soul.

*Fortissimo*! I put my arms out and fly while I spin.
I undulate my arms. I am a spinner, flying through

another night at the gym. I'm on my way to earning
angel wings that will take me into my afterlife.

## BEAUTY

Kids in the car, three different schools
for three different ages. 9 AM lecture and me,
the lecturer. Light streams through the side

windows of our front door. A bottle of *Pure
Chinese Red* nail polish flies from my hands
and shatters in a ruinous pattern across

an Italian marble floor. Each day another weight,
one after the other, it might have been
a severed artery, blood splatter from a heart,

mine, as I rush to the door, brush away
chips made by washing last night's dishes.
Something had to go, and it was this thing called

*perfection.* I no longer polish my nails. Now
nude, unvarnished as my emotions, a purity
so devoid of color, some might call it beauty.

# RÉSUMÉ

I am the caretaker of small things—darks
in one load, whites in another, sheets

by themselves. Only I open and close
windows, turn on and off fans,

dust, mop, hand out small portions
of food. Each person, each cat, a different

palate. I listen for wild birds, watch
a lavender sky fill to shades of blue.

An orange sun parades over fields
of hay now strewn with cut bales—

I see a hawk circle overhead as I open the door
to find two FBI agents in my doorway. I listen,

careful to say nothing of value, allow nothing
anyone would find interesting to spill out.

# HOMECOMING

85° and the sun weighs heavy on the back of my head.
Arriving home, I find the house locked, and me, without
a key. I travel from window to door to window, praying
for something to give. Nothing changes,

I stare in at the bedroom my stepdaughter sleeps in,
the same room she tells me she thinks about killing
herself. It looks friendly enough. Two easy chairs
in my office look inviting. Around back,

I push a patio table under a kitchen window. It's locked,
of course, and as I stand precariously balanced,
I look inside, imagine myself fixing ice tea, looking
out into the garden, then far off to the sea.

*Get hold of yourself*, I say, and crumple onto the table,
spread across its circumference, sobbing out years
of just scraping by and sacrifice, working two jobs
and school. I might have slept like that in the shade

dreaming about children and trouble, dancers, these two.
I climb down from that table, get a chair, and with force
I didn't know possible, I smash the window, and giving
no thought to shards of glass, walk straight through.

## LET IT RAIN WITH LOVE

A storm bears down on us from the west.
Church has just started, second verse
of the first hymn. I move into a pew
where people I know sit. They scrunch

together to make room. Just a couple
of minutes ago I was in the car traveling
back roads, past cows, horses, past
a gobble of wild turkeys, half-asleep

beside the two-lane byway, past a man
atop his ride-'um-cowboy mower,
past three boys on their bikes,
past the feed and grain store to church.

We call it a church, all of us, but it's hardly
more than a chapel, built in 1867. The rain
is earnest as we sit shoulder to shoulder,
filled with our sixty parishioners or so, not

counting Mildred's white toy poodle
she named Romeo. Alice Ann points to a place
in the hymnal, I pick up the melody, bow
my head at the correct time, kneel, make

the sign of the cross, say the Lord's Prayer.
Alice Ann shares her hymnal again, points
to the place where we need to be. In her
unsteady hands, I find forgiveness, loving

tenderness, faith in other people, hope
for our country, and inner peace. All
the blessings friendship provides
in this house of worship.

## LOOKING AT THE GROUND
## OUT A PASSENGER WINDOW OF OUR CAR

I sit here in a car waiting
for my husband's class to end,
a ruptured disc in my back.

I should at least know the name
for it, or perhaps a number, yes,
there are so many of them, I bet

discs have numbers. My aunt died
last night. She was a few months
shy of her hundredth birthday.

We were talking about her party
last week. *It's just a number,*
she said, *just another number.*

Everything has a name, or number,
I need to find out the number of
this ruptured disc. Might as well

call it by name as it intrudes
on my every move. At ninety-nine,
my aunt was the last of her generation.

She told me I was the only person left
alive from her youth. She was there
when I was born. There, too, my whole

life until now. I wait. Wind batters
the car. Rain falls lightly. Train tracks run
directly behind me. How is it possible

to adjust to such a loss with pain so constant.
Make friends with loss. Make friends with pain.
Make friends—rain hammers my car.

# A CONTINUOUS SPECTRUM OF COLOR

How is it possible not to feel forgiveness
when all our maples are opening red,

color of bravery, purity, happiness, heat,
and fire. Our river birches unfurl in green

as if Saint Patrick's Day was a holiday
they had to honor all spring. As dusk settles,

I smell yams baking. The sky fills with shades
of purple. Christopher Smart wrote

that purple is *black blooming*, but also it's the color
of royalty, imperialism, nobility, Easter,

Mardi Gras, wisdom, and rage. I know purple
will fade. Night will fall. I will lay my body down

and it will sleep. Ah, but my mind, now that
is a different color altogether. It continues…

forgive, forgive, until morning steals in
on rays of orange, color of healing, of power.

# THE LONGEST DAY

*I'm not happy*, I told a therapist, *I have no place to write.*
I didn't mention a friend said I could use her guesthouse,

a church down the road offered a pew, my husband said
I could use his studio, but those won't do. I need solitude,

no one waltzing through on the way to life. I can't write
with a cat in my lap, I've tried bedrooms, living room….

I would be happy with a place to write,
but it has to be the right place, no one smiling,

asking if I need a refill on my coffee. No!
I was brought up better than to say, *Just go away.*

So, tonight I've come to the fifth floor deck of our loft.
Far below, notes from a cello waft up and settle around me.

It's summer solstice, my birthday, damn near dark.
A bat just flew by and katydids are rubbing their wings

together or whatever they do to make that razor noise.
I find them distracting, but not quite as distracting

as a cat in my lap making little star feet all over my body.
My birthday, so many now, it's become an embarrassment.

I think about my mother, dead fifty years, how after the funeral,
her sister said, Y*our mother always was a turd of misery.*

I am *not* my mother.

# IN MY OWN VOICE

The rain has been with us so long
washing clean the surface streets
that cross, then cross again.
Cold Canyon Dry Creek
crosses Mulholland in Topanga
then again and again until
the Pacific Coast takes a stand:
This far, no farther.

I remember driving the only road
from Saint Ann's Bay to Kingston,
through the gaping mouth of a mountain
and yet, with solemn appetite,
it delivered me to a different coast.
Here, nothing but muddled dreams.
I thought I would be safe,
where I'd hoped rain

could wash my stained marriage clean.
To begin, and to begin again, to begin
each morning the way a conductor lifts his baton,
or the shopkeeper arrives, key in hand,
or the priest, again and again and again
reaches for the knob of a confessional,
or a mother, kneeling at the grave of her child,
I took a stand: *This far, no farther*.

## THE KNIFE

Wind blowing off the desert has shifted.
Currents gust from the north.
Soon, barred windows won't keep out cold.
I will rise from this marriage bed in search
of a knife, one to cut the cord of grief.
It must be honed so keen, it will put to rest
my husband's harsh breath that ignites like kerosene.

I am ashamed I haven't made a custard
to thicken this family. Ashamed too,
I've not been able to bear any children.
I am ashamed of my shoulders, suspended steel hangers,
work left undone, spots that lie unresolved,
and tears, running rampant until there is no surplus salt.
However, shame does not render absolution.

This I know: I wander dark halls
with sharp edges, and I'm sliced at every turn.
I carry dreams in the thin shafts of my hair,
now a knife, hidden and waiting.
I'll wait until dawn of the next full moon.
I'll wait, savoring deposits of salt.
I'll not wait much longer.

## SPILT MILK

I've heard it all my life—someone's mother
saying, *No sense crying over spilt milk.*
But after two cups of my special blend
of coffee and milk, and while making the third,
the last of the milk misses the cup
and spreads across my counter in a whitewash.

I can't stop crying—how long has such grief
been waiting? How is it that I woke at five,
showered, made the bed and fed cats,
like it was any other morning?
Now, grief drives cats under the bed.
In time, I too work one arm and a shoulder

into their dusky cave with its heavy
unblinking stillness. I wish to be small—
small as a cat so that I might curl under the bed—
blue carpeting my cushion, underside of the mattress
my white sky. Anyone who stopped would frown.
I couldn't blame them—

a small alabaster body in a cave,
kitchen tiles glazed white,
and grief—such grief,
free to roam from room to room
waiting to be fed.

# A PREDICTION OF ARMAGEDDON

Ships lined up obscure the view
of Catalina. My window opens
to dark clouds that roll and twist.

There must be a school of fish
just offshore. Gulls are circling
and diving, four or more at a time.

Workmen next door make haste
to finish the roof. They call to one
another above the din of crashing

waves. I make out the words *must*
and *watertight*. The men stare with
awe at the sky's brooding turmoil.

Soon, whatever is done will be all
there is time for. The rain will rage
against our plate glass and obliterate

my view of ships, the island, waves,
even the building under construction.
Men will drive away, truck windows

fogged with their hurried breath.
Today's sunrise was gold and russet.
Venus, jewel of the sky, lay over lunar alps.

I can no longer keep myself from singing.
Not softly or under my breath
but with full, round sounds

that boom from my throat. I sing
like a crazy woman, while birds perch
under a canopy of trees. They listen!

## CHANGE OF SEASON

Lately I haven't wanted to leave the house.
I've been content as grass growing,
wild with color,
and deeply rooted as an old tree
with new leaves that sprout for spring.

I long for nothing—
dream of just where I am,
worry over my indoor plants
and camellias coloring the front porch,
roses gathering strength from winter.

Oh, did I mention that I saw a coyote
walking right down the middle of a road
yesterday at four in the afternoon? And
that it rained as I woke today? Did I say
that I put a log in my fireplace,

when the embers turned bright orange,
I fed them all the court documents,
except for that final decree,
and watched as the whole pile turned
to ash? It burned bright as a sunny day.

# THE OLD LIFE

Sunday morning, far off, a wailing siren,
whistle of a train I have yet to see, although
I feel its timbre trembling the ground.

A dog barks, peacocks cry out,
a bobwhite quail tells me everything he knows,
while a rabbit silently inspects my flower beds.

There is a starling in trouble with a pair
of sparrows, who give chase, and church bells
ring every hour. I must be mistaken to think this,

but I'm sure I can hear grass growing,
how it springs from the moist depth of earth.
My two cats lie in the sun.

All this is a relief, after I woke from a night
of dreams about surgery, eviction, and
thugs breaking in through the front door.

How I wish for my mind of the past washed
clean. I need to know that at long last,
my life is just about perfect.

Yet, that old life, yes, the old, old life,
still begs to be heard, still asks for,
but doesn't give a moment of peace.

# INTO THAT BLACK NIGHT

Some days I wake just knowing what kind of day it's going to be I look out the window in hope of seeing something that's going to prove me wrong but instead I see an arrow of Canada geese flying south I have a choice of oatmeal or cat food for breakfast so I cook oatmeal and take it out to the back steps I think about how one cat is still asleep and one sits outside with me looking up into the tree at a squirrel looking back at her while the third cat wanted out at two this morning so instead of just opening a door and letting him out how I tossed him out to give him a head start into that black night and if the little bugger doesn't stop waking me at two in the morning he could find himself an outdoor cat instead of making himself comfy all day on my down comforter I know he's out there catting around like maybe the vet didn't quite get everything I leave for work ten minutes late and by the time I get to the freeway cars are lined up bumper to bumper which makes me nervous until  I see the problem is just ahead I feel relief until my car reaches the trouble spot and a police motorcycle lies sideways and twisted across a lane of traffic and a man in uniform has been tossed to the side of the road like a discarded mannequin and nobody seems in a hurry to get help It is difficult to just drive by seeing the officer's head twisted at an odd angle and one leg has a crazy flare I wonder if he is married and if his wife knows or maybe his mother and now I'm not mad or nervous anymore just sad for us all because life is so hard I just wonder at how one minute everything sounds like it's going to be okay then bam like yesterday when this guy I've been dating for seven months calls to say that he is having a problem with our relationship and that he's scared because he thinks I'm getting involved like it's up to me to tell this jerk that relationships move in one direction or the other and I think he's old enough to know the way it works I get to work and my boss can't see me because he had to fly to San Jose for some emergency I feel like maybe I'm turning into an emergency I go back home and write rejection letters all afternoon thinking how these people send work out and how it must feel getting so many rejection letters I know that's the way it is because their work is just so bad I try to balance my checkbook which hasn't balanced properly for a year now but I pay bills anyway and near as I can figure it leaves me with $47.36 which isn't enough to buy groceries for the next two weeks so it looks like I'll be eating oatmeal until my next paycheck That's when my friend Stephanie calls to inform me Mercury is retrograde like I didn't already know I go downstairs to get my tape recorder out of the car because Yusef Komunyakaa asked me to make him a tape of me reading some of his poems and I drop the darn thing on the way back upstairs smashing it all to smithereens I don't know what to do because if there isn't money for food I surely don't have money to fix the thing or buy another plus the cord on the vacuum refuses to wind itself back inside so I take the thing apart and as the last screw comes out the motor flies all over the kitchen I know I'll never get it back together I look at the kitchen clock which says it's only 3 PM but I think I'd like a martini and I can't help but wonder what a nice girl like me is doin' with problems like these I fix a cup of coffee then decide to add sugar because sometimes that's the only thing you can do to sweeten things up.

# CONTINUATION

Ask me what I am
and I will point to fruit
ripened by sun, fully exposed

as I watch three chipping sparrows
build a nest in a palm frond.
I imagine the third bird

to be a brother-in-law
in the construction business,
accustomed to couples building

featherbed grass woven nests.
He will leave, I think,
when the job is done.

Sunday—I wake at seven,
and think of my husband,
now not my husband,

and wonder how long it takes
before I stop thinking of him
as my husband.

Later I walk in a garden.
Here, the fallen fruit
returns to earth.

Some things have the nerve
to start again: roses,
sweet alyssum, and mint.

## SURVIVAL I

Daddy was raised up like a ragamuffin.
Mama, she was born having convulsions.

Neither one of them able to take care of
themselves much less each other,

plus two offspring. But we kids made it,
somehow, and today, I'm hunkered down

in a closet, away from any windows,
smack dab in the center of our house,

waiting for an all-clear from a tornado warning.
And what is it that occupies my thoughts?

I'm trying to remember how many acres Edward Abbey
wrote of owning in *Desert Solitaire*, 33,000, I think.

## DUTCH MASTERS

I've not mentioned this 'til now, but the night
my father died, the hospital gave me some things.

Besides the clothes he'd worn, there was a cigar box—
nothing much—a man sleeping in doorways travels light.

When I opened the box, his Social Security card was on top,
ragged around the edges.

Under the card, receipts from a paint store,
and my wedding picture—whiskey stained, corners bent

from being propped up against one thing or another.
Yet, there I sat on a Louis XIV divan—so young,

white gown spread to show off lace and seed pearls.
There was a picture of my brother too,

taken when he was about twelve, one knee planted
on home plate, a fierce eye to the camera.

At the bottom, three quarters, a dime, and a 1949
fifty-cent piece. *That's all she wrote*, he would have said.

*You live your heaven and hell right here on earth, Kid,*
*pay some attention to the details.*

## OUT OF NOWHERE

    this morning, the memory of hiding in a closet,
seven years old, my father in the kitchen of that
small California Court apartment, past midnight.
Across the center pathway, all the lights
of other houses are dark, and him,
with yet another freshly poured drink,
talking to dead men in his unit, back
riding waves toward Omaha Beach,
those rolling waves, the boat about to fall open,
that trembling boat—sweet mother of Jesus,
into cold water they went,
rifles above their heads. Have mercy, pray
for us all in the hour of our need.

## SURVIVAL II

Rain falling is not a judgment.
That's what we learned in our parents' house

as we grew. That's all that was required,
we survive and grow. We were told

we had it all: brains and looks. My brother said
even as a child, he knew

there was a man inside of him. We stayed alive
through the botch our parents made

of absolutely everything. We stayed alive
to grow into the people we knew we already were.

## LIVING WITH SOUNDS OF MOURNING

Death is on the other side of the river today,
taking two of my friends in a week.
My upper lip quivers. *When did that start?*
I grit my teeth and it stops, but my jaw

starts to hurt so I relax, and the quiver returns.
*Can anyone see,* I think, and lift a finger to the spot,
but my hand is unsteady. Yesterday I heard a child
screaming as if she was being murdered.

Then I saw a man calmly pushing a stroller,
the child slumped over a tray exhausted
by her ordeal. The father's face was blank,
perhaps wondering how this came to pass,

this child, conceived in love, and now, makes
the light fixtures shatter to dust with the
volume of her frustration. How are we to think
about such sorrow when we are yet alive?

I lift both hands to my face, trace the orbs
of my eyes, with my palms, cup both my cheeks.
I look into the darkest place of myself,
then part my hands to daylight.

## CHILDREN ARE NOT SUPPOSED TO DIE
## BEFORE THEIR PARENTS

She manages like a woman living someone else's life
and finds a navy blue summer suit a couple of decades old,
way, way in the back of her closet. The skirt actually fits.

The jacket is short-sleeved, with huge shoulder pads,
a look that may have been striking twenty years before,
but today, looks like a throwback from something

out of *Vogue* magazine. Shoes would be a problem,
she knows, *Oh, who cares,* she says to no one, and digs
through a stack of boxes she doesn't remember buying

to finds a pair of navy sandals. *Surely,*
she thinks, *these must belong to someone else.*
She stuffs tissues in her purse, just in case

she weakens for a moment, but anger tends to be
all consuming, and she doesn't think she'll need them
for years perhaps, when tears are all that's left.

# A DOCUMENTARY ON MORNING

The tide forces itself against a sea wall.
Gulls have taken up their post. Geese fly north,
starlings in circles. Divers are in murky waters
for the third day in a row following police boats,

their nets drag the channel. I climb higher
to the loft from where the next step
surely must be heaven. I don't ask myself
any questions. I'm not looking for answers.

I am greeted by still air, imposing fog,
and a chill that crept in over the long night.
I have carried with me an unopened envelope.
I know what it contains, pictures

of my dead daughter's child, a girl,
Genevieve, her father has named her.
I sit without trembling, my head tilted back
and watch an overhead fan punish air.

## DUSTING

I think I've begun to heal.
Days pass,

sometimes in whole hours
without drawing a ragged

breath in grief. I can be engaged
in the single act of…

oh, let's say dusting,
thinking about

nothing at all save the weather,
or I need to check

the birdfeeder. Beds
get made,

meals get served, clothes
get washed,

books are consumed,
and my heart

beats steady in its small
satchel inside my chest.

## WHAT HAVE I DONE WITH LOVE

Morning rises, sun sets. I hold my breath, become still
and look over the countryside. Before the arrow flies,
before I shoot, I see myself as a farmer, as a hunter,
as the caretaker of bones. I have learned all things
go into the earth; all that I am, I take with me.
All that I am, I give away.

It came into my mind that no one had written
what was already planted deep in the ground.
If I put it down in the bones of words, it becomes
an arrow into a heart. Above ground, it would
come again as what I hunted, and wherever
it was, would fall.

## MASTER PLAN

The maple's bright leaves wave from the roadside
and I'm off to target practice, where I'll learn how
to cock my newly acquired twenty-gauge shotgun,

how to bring it up from my hip
Chuck Connors-style in *The Rifleman*.
I can do this! Go to the closet,

cock shotgun, call 911, announce
in a loud voice that although I am
armed and a marksman, I fear

for my life. Listen, if someone wants
to mess with me after all that,
why, he'd deserve what comes next.

But, oh, what a mess. I hate to think about it.
I think I could convince an intruder,
in fact I know I could, that it would

be much better for all concerned if he'd
leave now by the same way he'd entered,
*I'll stay right here in the closet,* I'll say,

*the police won't come for another minute, run,*
*quick—run!* I'll ask him to think it over,
*Does anyone survive birdshot at talking range?*

# REGRETTABLE INVESTMENT

The front sprinklers go on at 5 AM.
An hour later, they have watered
the grass, sidewalk, curb, and washed
clean the street, which has turned
into a river wide enough

to carry a canoe. The water runs
by our neighbor's house, then his
neighbor's, runs fast into the circle
of the cul-de-sac. Mike Burke,
from the city, was by yesterday

sometime. He left a checklist
at the door: Valve #1 held at 9.6
PSID- Valve #2 back pressure test
is closed tight at 8.6- Relief Valve
is open at 3.4 PSID, and you can only

imagine how my heart fluttered
with the news that line pressure is Not
Applicable. The Shutoff Valve is closed
tight at 9.6- and the Backflow device,
well, let's hear it from the choir, it passed!

Dear Mr. Burke:
The only thing not explained in detail
is why our water bill was $183.27
for this past month, and how to adjust
the bloody system from forming a river,
wade-worthy. Although I do love seeing
happy children, their water polo games
each afternoon in the cul-de-sac seem
more than my budget can manage.
In closing, is there something you would
recommend for the mold that grows in
large patches around our flower beds?

Most sincerely,
Stellasue Lee

## ANYPLACE BUT HERE

Daybreak! An earth digger worries morning.
I'll call the city today! There are rules: 7 AM,

they can't start before. If I had my way,
they would be gone for good. No reason

for a double-wide road leading to a new school.
There would be no new school. Once we'd arrived

in Spring Hill, I wanted a new rule, one that states:
*no more building, no more traffic.* From now on

just these cows, horses, birds, and buffalo. I read
a songwriter, known well enough that what he said

got into print, told how he purchased 30 acres,
and moved to Middle Tennessee. He woke up that

first morning to find Saturn building a new
production plant adjacent to his backyard. Imagine!

He didn't even unpack, just put his house up for sale
and moved back to Los Angeles. So don't come here,

not even for a visit. Don't even think about moving
here. The landscape is ugly. People are unfriendly.

Cows moo all the time. Children play everywhere.
Everything is green. It's perpetually spring.

Stars litter the sky. Anyway, it's shocking to think
just anyone could fall in love with a shaggy buffalo.

## PUGET SOUND

Nine days walking wooded paths, sleeping in rooms
built during WWII meant for officers who thought

Japanese submarines would slide though dark
of night by way of Puget Sound. I've explored

bunkers and cannons still in place, ravishingly
abundant woods, beaches of driftwood and shells.

We queue up three times a day for meals. That first
night was grilled salmon caught that day,

served on a bed of wild rice with vegetables plucked
from the ground that very morning. Wild-berry pie.

Nine evening meals later, *fresh* no longer applied,
and Milo, our chef, looms behind steam tables

just waiting for negative comments, and when it's said,
when someone can't stand it any longer, Milo's face

turns red, the appearance of having been boiled,
his eyes the color of Cognac set ablaze, his mouth

pinched with cayenne, he screams, "You Goddamned
writers—you all think you're some kind of Picasso!"

# TWO
## LIKE A PALETTE OF RAIN CLOUDS,
### EYES THE COLOR OF YOUNG RICE

*"In ancient
times
cats were
worshipped
as gods;
they have
not forgotten
this."*

–Terry Pratchett

# RAIN

## 1

This is how I imagined living in the canyon would be,
owls hooting well into night.
Come morning—I'm awakened by a pulsating,
deep and disturbing.
I think it must be my own heart,
then realize it comes from far off—
a car radio perhaps, turned full volume,
someone coming through the canyon
lonely, bent on waking everyone.

## 2

A man sits at the base of the canyon
with his dog.
They both look homeless.
He wears a poncho and a wide-brimmed hat,
carries a sign all through the long summer:
*Why lie    I need* ♥
Once, waiting for the light to change,
I saw him walk to the doorway of a bank
and relieve himself,
then give the dog's leash a terrible yank.

3

My neighbor is a man in his forties,
tall, with a light complexion.
Every time he leaves his apartment, he starts whistling
as if he is happy or friendly,
but he isn't either of these two things.
I think his whistling is a cover-up.
My bedroom is just above the garages,
and as he lifts the garage door just under my bed,
I feel his anger in the vibration of the wood.
At five minutes to five this morning,
I hear him whistling, "Michael, Row the Boat Ashore."

4

Rain pounds the roof.
I imagine I'm in a rainforest.
At seventeen minutes past 4 AM,
the canyon is hushed in fog.
On my way home last night,
the homeless man and his dog
lay curled in a doorway of the bank.
My neighbor is away on business.
I listen to rain fall with the same steady rhythm
as the beating of my heart.
When the cat comes to snuggle,
I stuff him under the comforter,
draw my knees up around his body.

## HALLOWEEN

Nothing is real in October!
There is a cat on the roof—
my cat.

He sits there watching me on the porch—
maybe thinking
*my woman.*

Either way—

the two of us
loving the wild light wind makes
moving through trees,
casting shadows on the patio
then drenching us in bright light.

Leaves turn the color
of pomegranates.

Birds call back and forth
busy with business of the day.

Nothing is real
but this savage joy
in a world I have made for myself
and is as arguable as color
flung from a palette
on a morning
when the wind is up.

# MEMORY OF RED

A lawnmower's steady hum,
sun playing in the canopy of trees,
then silence—almost painful, until
a bird's full-throated song starts.

This feels familiar as I fall asleep and dream,
something I've dreamt before—
cats, a house full of them—on the sofa,
every chair, table, kitchen counter,

laundry basket, everywhere I turn.
I pick up the black one, a sleek beauty,
open a door and tell it, *Go home!*
Next, a long-haired tricolor, I tell it too,

*Go home!* But when it comes to the red cat,
candy-apple, four-alarm-fire red,
with canary yellow stripes that blaze back
from the corner of each eye—now here's

a prize! I'm holding her up rejoicing
when my eyes blink open on the present world,
one painfully lacking a red and yellow cat,
a dull, simple world.

## PARALLEL UNIVERSES

Saturday morning, like the old days when I wasn't working.
Blackbirds plague our bird feeder. Cowbirds gather

in a field nearby. Roses wither in sun as neighborhood children
run through sprinklers in underwear, screaming in delight.

It's 7 AM. Our mother rabbit feeds her young that are still safe
in the warren. Two cats hang out with me in bed. My husband,

the photographer, is upstairs in his darkened post-production
studio where he sees nothing of our lives. He is at work on a new

image from the series he has named *Farmer in the Dell.*
Scrupulously, he observes every detail of the picture while I,

downstairs in the light of a real world, observe with accuracy
each astonishing detail of our temporal everyday life.

## EIGHT THOUSAND SEVEN HUNDRED
## AND SIXTY GOOD DAYS

In early spring, many years ago, I woke only to remain
in bed. So pretty a day, so much to do. I was sick,
sick to the point of dying sick, so sick I didn't care.

The week before, I had broken off an engagement,
returned the ring, told him I'd rather live alone,
now I was sick, three days sick, and sick of being sick.

The doorbell rang and I thought it was angels singing.
I woke and stumbled toward the sound,
fragile, feverish, heart pounding from effort.

The man I said I didn't want stood at my door with a kitten,
tiny thing, a small blue box with some sand,
and a few cans of food. He thrust the mewing baby

into my arms, set supplies inside the door, and left,
turned and left, without uttering a word, left me
with this living thing to care for. It was two more days

before the fever broke, two days of outlandish dreams,
sweats, and incoherent murmurs. Two days before
I came into myself enough to notice the kitten

snuggled beside me. Two days before I woke to my life
and all that came true over the next twenty-four years.
Twenty-four years of constant companionship and love.
His name was Rex. He was a king among cats.

# LOOSE LIMBED AND WEEPING BY THE WATER'S EDGE

I woke tired this morning;
teary, even. Later, Tennyson,

the cat we just adopted,
walked by my chair, tail up,

close enough to show
he's already come to expect

my hand to fall for the sleek
sable of his black length.

Now he jumps into the companion chair
to be near. He seems to enjoy

the pen's movement,
my reflective posture.

There is an early morning sun.
It streaks across the room,

wind ripples the surface of water
that surrounds this house.

For a moment, I am grateful
then, tears again. I miss

our old cat, gone seven months,
who knew all of my moods

and never minded one of them.
He left me while I held him

in my arms as I had
for the past twenty years,

trusting that very moment,
too, was part of our whole.

# BEYOND THE PADDOCK, STABLE, RING

I can't tell you what heartache came up in me
on the drive to Chapel Hill, and after, standing

among horses, each one clearly positioning
closer to have her head rubbed. I felt the warmth

of hide against my open palm, brush of tail
across my hand, heard birds call as light turned

soft as flannel. Early morning does this these first
days of fall. And later, another overwhelming

urge to cry while I sat in the gazebo listening
to acorns drop from a scarlet oak, a tinny sound

against the roof, making me think of rain falling
on a closed coffin until I was unable to see

through tears. The old dog, the one we call Robin,
for he is very brave and ferociously protective,

came into the gazebo to lay his head in my lap.
And if he could, he'd attack whatever old grief

haunts me still, but as it is, he can only comfort,
and so too, bear the weight of what he can't see

yet knows surrounds us, the heartache that gnaws
at my edges, nibbles away daily at this heart of mine.

# SOFT TOUCH

This cat presses his body against mine,
stretches out along the length of my leg,

ankle to hip bone. He was in a cage at
an open-air market, huge yellow eyes full

of fright. He was mine, and I was his.
A blue jay peers in as it sits on our patio railing

until he finds us within. He wants his morning
allotment of peanuts, so I put my journal aside,

get up and walk to the kitchen. The cat follows.
We get peanuts, open the door and toss them

one by one. Once, the bird flew away, but now
he stays and watches me. When I've thrown

the last one, he sets about the task of collecting
them. Doves watch also. I'm ashamed to tell you this,

but I've allowed a whole box of sesame crackers
to stale, just so I could crumble and toss them too.

# MAYBE SHE DREAMS OF FIELDS

Kaylee comes, head down when we whistle.
She mews like a newborn.

I don't remember why my husband
started to whistle for her, or even

why she responded, but she shows up,
jumps into the lap of whoever called her,

circles twice, then eases herself down, always
with a deep sigh and silent passing of wind.

These moments generate inactivity for me
as she dreams whatever it is kittens dream.

Whiskers twitch, ears swivel, and there is
an occasional shake of her small and delicate paw.

# LIKE A PALETTE OF RAIN CLOUDS,
## EYES THE COLOR OF YOUNG RICE

She is silver, signifying wealth.
Each blue hair
is tipped with shine,

and she lets me know she thinks
I'm a dud, even though I'm the one
who put a toy mouse stuffed

with catnip into the bathtub
so that she could slip, paw, tumble
and chase it all about.

She chews each corner
of my journal, has been known
to stick her nose in my coffee,

fish shrimp out of a temporarily
unattended bowl of steaming
Top Ramen, and steal

anything she has a mind to steal
from my kitchen counter.
She has the mentality of

a five-year-old with an awful
case of the terrible twos.
Kaylee is a Korat. Google that,

then be filled with wonder,
dear reader, at the mental
instability of this author.

# HER HONEY-BUNCH, GUM-DROP, SWEETIE-PIE IS GONE

Saturday, no calls I have to make, no plans
of any kind, just this cat, looking deeply into my eyes,
questioning why my husband isn't here—

and if she could, she would order me to bring him back.
When I try to hold her, comfort her, she gives me
a stiff-legged response, pushing away, and looks
down her nose at me, her eyes wide, clearly
questioning my presumption that she wants to be held.

> *No!—No holding! Go to airport!*
> *Bring him back!*

Every piece of fur points in that direction.
I make breakfast, eat, shower, dress.
I find her in a closet, face burrowed deep
in his shoe. She doesn't even bother to acknowledge
my presence. Her alpha male is gone—her main
squeeze, schnooky lumps, gum-drop-cuddle-bear,
Lancelot, heartthrob, big daddy-yum-yum
is gone, along with his lap, gone—

and, since I am the one who is in attendance
to all her kitty needs, she blames me for his absence.

Later, she digs up a plant, throws up on my most
expensive Chinese carpet, cuffs poor Tennyson
after he washes her face and pushes a kibble in her
direction, offers to share his place in the sun.

Tennyson, the perfect Tuxedo cat, he accepts
it all, loves her anyway, as we all do. Kaylee,
Kaylee, Kaylee, I want to coo, Pretty Girl,

your daddy will be home on Thursday, but she
is back in the closet, sitting on a shelf below
his shirts, her head stretched up in a whirl
of fabric, her tail drumming against a finished
wood shelf, lost in her kitty world of mourning.

## LETTER TO MY MOTHER
### WHOM I BLAMED FOR ABSOLUTELY EVERYTHING

You've been gone fifty years, Mother.
I no longer blame you, and I miss that.
This business of accepting responsibility

myself for every little thing is difficult.
So when things go awry, my husband
and I blame Kaylee, mischievous thing

that she is. She handles it well, much
better than you ever did. As long as she
can jump up on our kitchen counter

and supervise my opening a can of cat food
into a clean bowl twice a day, she's good.
She is independent, sweet and funny,

as you were, a true nonconformist,
just like you. She is most beautiful, a show-
stopper. She has star quality, like you.

## ALMOST DARK,
### AND BARN SWALLOWS WANT TO REST

Our street is flooded. Monsoon-like rain pools
across blacktop reflecting only gray air

and soft light. Pink and white crepe myrtles
bow from the weight of it all. Even an 8 PM

train whistle crossing under an overpass sounds
muffled, as if underwater. Cows stand in this

long shower, temperature just perfect
for a cow. No flies, yet plenty of grass, while

their young enjoy daylight, blink away water
from their new summer eyes. It's grand weather

for ducks. Trees no longer stark, although
I do see one that is without any sort of canopy.

It's ripe to be felled by lightning, but not today,
there is just rain. I'll remain on the porch

until guilt drives me inside. The barn swallows
circle, wanting to come in from the rain.

*Forgive me, little birds, and understand, I paid*
*for this porch, its easy chairs, footstool,*

*the pillars you are so fond of camping out on*
*during the long night. Come in, come on ahead,*

*call it a day and fly in if you wish. It's safe.*
*I'm going to stay just a while longer.*

# WAKING UP WITH RAYMOND CARVER
## AND JACK GILBERT

My husband brings me coffee, but the steaming
cup sits until eventually it grows cold, I am so
intent on reading every word, how Jack's failing

marriage came so successfully to an end and
Ray's children making all the mistakes he made.
My two cats lounge in bed with me. Although

Tennyson did some egregious thing to Kaylee
last night and her scream, followed by a hiss,
got me thinking about life, and I remembered

what I had wanted. I wanted everything clean
and neat, freshly washed, pressed, in its place,
sane, yes, sane, and what had I discovered,

well, life gets messy, sometimes very messy,
and you learn to love it, or it buries you,
neat and clean and six feet under.

## POSTSCRIPT TO LOSS

Bird flutters around the front porch. Among
the items Bird inspects is a pair of shoes—

mine, kept by the door for outdoor wear,
run-to-the-mailbox shoes, get-paper shoes,

take-out-the-trash shoes, garden shoes—
and briefly, I wonder if Bird is thinking about

building her nest in said shoes. Knitting
twigs through the long laces, binding things,

a nest made into a stronghold,
a regular fortress for nestlings. Bird finishes

her inspection before she flies into the eaves—
*Good choice, Bird, eaves are built to last.*

No matter how strong you build, I think,
you can't always keep your children safe.

And even the best of homes
can't restore their dead. I know.

*Leave the shoes, dear Bird, build your home*
*in the eaves. Bring me new life.*

## WASHING THE FLOOR

I get down on my hands and knee, but my floor
never seems to come completely clean. Mop and
mop, and still I find cat hair, black, like my Sari,
and gray, fringed with white, my Bob's.

Long strands gracefully arranged on the floor,
s-shaped: my first name's first letter. Across the room,
brown and white fur clings in a clump to a Lalique vase.
The grandfather clock chimes 4:30 AM.

Now the floor has been washed twice. By the time
6 o'clock chimes, I've done the floor four times more.
Even in sleep, I'm obsessive. One cat stretches out
on the dining room table, another is curled in a basket

on top of a bureau. A cat I've never seen before
is in the seat of a Queen Anne chair.
Another one drapes along the sofa's back.
Two more cats huddle over the food dish.

One bites and chews, waits for the other to follow suit.
Five more cats are asleep on my bed.
I open a closet and three cats jump out,
veer around the corner and race down the hall.

With this many cats, I dream of finding another place
to live, but before I can reach a door, four cats roll
into a ball that becomes the wheels of my car.
I drive off intending never to come back.

What must it be to wash a floor just once a week?
That's when I wake and realize the floor needs washing.

# THIRTEEN MONTHS AND COUNTING

Birds wake me each morning. We are here for such a short time,
and already I know I will miss living on the water. Days have passed
since I've seen a great blue heron. Yesterday, a solo pelican
sat on a dock with a dozen young gulls who waited for nothing
more than their white belly feathers to grow.

Three goslings hang out on a dock across a narrow channel,
almost as large as their mother. They turn as she turns,
lower their heads as if to appear smaller, make begging
sounds as she brings food. When she flies away, they stand tall,
stretch their wings, waddle along the dock on webbed tippy toes.

This marina could break your heart with its floating docks, smart
architectural homes, eucalyptus and pines anchored to earth.
Experts predict the sea will rise fifty feet from global warming.
The marina will be submerged. These boats will be unmoored
and abandoned, like so many yearlings their mothers drove off.

I sit on a balcony overlooking boats, kayakers, and birds as they
glide by. A ring-necked dove nests in rafters. I listen as the grandfather clock gathers strength to strike the hour. Light seeps
into a morning sky. Another perfect day, but I can't stop myself
from counting, thirteen months before we must leave this place.

## STREET CATS

Cats in Key West don't look well cared for.
They appear small, withdrawn, philosophical even.
They know there is a fine for disturbing
a chicken, but no such rule to safeguard the cats.

They come to me after a couple of slow
blinks, still present, knowing who they are,
loving themselves when no one shines
the light of friendship on them. I want

to love them all, but they are accustomed
to seeing people walk away. Their meetings
are so temporary, a street leading to another
street, and all the streets leading away.

How do I communicate that this isn't the way
it's supposed to be? They look at the chickens
who haven't the sense God gave a turnip,
but strut around free and full of chicken nonsense.

*Dearest cats, I will take all of you home with me*
*here, here in my heart. You are loved and beautiful.*
I will forever cherish the nameless brown cat,
the one who rolled over to show me his tummy.

And the gray cat that gave me a head butt. The yellow
tabby that fell on my feet and comforted herself
by rubbing her head on my shoes. You are here,
here in my heart and mind, beloved.

# TEARING OPEN EACH DAY

Rain, with punishing intensity, gives way to a torrent
of water that runs down our street. Neighbors tell me

to secure all windows, wind will follow. I worry
about our newly hatched finches, our robin. Two days

that robin has hopped back and forth along the footprint
of our house, while its mother is kept busy bringing it food.

The fledgling flaps its wings expectantly, but nothing happens.
Its mother and I both know the hazards of a night on the ground.

Late in the afternoon, I speak with my husband who
is in Los Angeles waiting for an earthquake while I remain

in Tennessee avoiding tornadoes. Nightfall and the cats
and I crawl into bed. Little Kaylee wants under the comforter,

but Tennyson chooses his spot at the foot of my bed—
a stone gargoyle watches through the long, ravaged night.

## INSIDE THE NATURE OF THINGS

There's only one squirrel feasting in the branches
  high in the canopy
of my oak this morning. I love that old tree.
It presides      yes      presides
over the yard    as a priestly thing—
a thing to pay homage to, something reverential
  to hold
in highest regard.                  So it is
each morning I sit in the red chair        cats at my feet
happy            I think,    the day started
door open to the patio            cats feeding,
  flowers in full bloom.
I too    am happy                feel blessed, in fact.

Once I saw a squirrel drop from one of the tallest
branches—fell through the air and hit the ground
with a thud. I could hear it                feel
  it in the ground, that thud.
I know what it's like                to have the wind knocked
out of me        know that stunned feeling
for months                undressing all aspects of tragedy
  and then                the climb
sure-footed with a firmer grip on life
some              odd mercy      at having come through it all.

## CROWS

Crows are usually plentiful along my street
dropping nuts from up high
then swooping down to sort through what remains
but on this day
for no good reason I can think of
I am watching from the window
thinking how strange
not one of those large blackbirds
is anywhere in sight
when a woman,
leading the teeniest dog
whose long shaggy fur gives the illusion
of a mop skittering along the street
must have felt a tug
as one of the crows
swoops out of the sky
and snatches the dog and leash
right out of the woman's clutches
leaving us both open mouthed
and staring at the early morning sky
and the last I see of either the crow
or the dog
is one final glimpse of the two
flying directly into a rising sun
coming out of the canyon
past trees and the hilly countryside
just beyond the great city of Los Angeles.

# ONCE IN A BLUE MOON

*It was a dark and stormy night*, I thought, and smiled,
the very words take away all fear, but there were lightning

strikes, hubristic claps of thunder, and you might say
that we were tucked safely in our beds—for it was indeed

the night before Christmas. Morning rose bright and clear,
actually warm. With New Year's looming, I placed an order

for forty-eight packages of Greenies, which given judiciously, equates
to two packages per cat, per month at $2.95 each. This adds up

to $11.80. Now, let's multiply by twelve, and that comes to
$141.60 a year, which doesn't include food, litter, and shots.

After placing the order, I went over to the Cattery, where
I was forced to explain all this to Issy and Pumpkin,

just eleven weeks old, sitting in a small cage waiting for
a *Forever Home*. I want to give them that home,

such dear little faces, might even convince the two I have
to accept them, but with no increase from Social Security,

I wouldn't be able to afford the Greenies.
So much for the magic of *once in a blue moon*.

# SUNSET BEACH, CALIFORNIA

I have to hand it to the oven manufacturer
of this Regency VSA Touch Control. Top
of the line, like everything else in this place.

But where the time should appear, the display
flashes HELP—my wish exactly. I looked
for a dialog button, something, you understand,

but there is nothing that guides me how to be
of service. Its silent cry blinks through my dreams.
The landlord has been informed. I'm sure I mentioned

the oven, along with the TV that doesn't work,
washer/dryer, vacuum, dishwasher, A/C,
three of five stove burners. I should put a warning

on the toilet seats (they can throw you
if you don't pay attention), and we are paying
dearly for this ocean view, two fireplaces,

private beach—location, location, and yes,
this place deserves one more *location*. My cat
sits on the counter and looks quizzically

at the flashing plea. She knows what it means to need
help—and she would help, but as things stand,
neither of us can do a thing. So I open windows

to cool air as it blows off the water, take my
laundry to a fluff and fold, read more, live rich,
eat poor, and enjoy my vacation.

## BACON

Here come our two cats for my breakfast,
but I am not eating, rather looking down,
making the pen move with familiar loops
and a certain steady slide across the page.

Cats bore easily when they see that ink smears
and doesn't taste a thing like chicken. So
the leader pushes her nose into an African violet,
which I can't allow. Given her way, she will destroy

leaves and get soil all over the table, along with
pretty purple flowers. I pluck her from the pot,
but not before a clump of dirt hits the table
and she finds it didn't taste a thing like turkey,

which was what she had on her little kitty brain.
Off the two go to explore the kitchen, tails entwined,
leaving me in solitude with nothing more than
steam rising from the electric facility at the end

of Korean War Veterans Bridge and downtown
Nashville waking to another day of rain.
Now I hear the cats discussing how bacon is cured
and the virtue of Costco's brand, Kirkland,

fully cooked, naturally wood smoked, thick cut,
microwaveable, pre-sliced, ready in a mere 55 seconds,
reminding me we can have bacon for breakfast.
P.S. and by the way, I cook one piece for each cat.

# FAREWELL! THOU ART TOO DEAR FOR MY POSSESSING
—William Shakespeare

*Window gazing*, I call it, while I
mindlessly fold laundry. Spring creeps
into morning below the window

where needles of underbrush quiver. Just at the base
of a river birch planted last year, a tiny head
pokes through the leaves, followed by a body

the size of a fingerling potato.
Three more baby rabbits come forth
out of the ground, so emaciated

their legs can barely support them.
Something must have happened to the doe.
Had they not been desperate,

had they not been starving, they would
have stayed in that snug burrow.
I buy fresh bunches of gourmet lettuce,

heap them on a platter, julienne carrots,
mix in a few blueberries, slice strawberries,
steal a fistful of hay from a pasture

down the road. Those bony little darlings
grow fat as tennis balls, scamper through bushes
dormant all winter, and then our bunnies

leave. My husband and I stand with our cats
at the window. I tell them our rabbits have gone
for their baccalaureates. Days later, I am folding

clothes again, window gazing, and I see one bunny
hop along below the window, as if to say, *Yes,*
*this is where I was born, this is where I grew.*
*Yes, life is good.*

# THEORY OF FLUX

An A/C cycles on/off. Patti's cat sits
at a back door, looks through glass

for deer or raccoons, wild things
along the banks of a Harpeth tributary

running through Patti's back property.
Her other cat runs up and down

the hall making wild animal sounds.
I like being at Patti's house. It feels

more permanent than my own home
where my husband works with a crew

of women to weed through his studio.
Heraclitus, the philosopher, said

*There is nothing permanent except change.*
I stand very still and wait for what is to come.

If this were a movie script, I would
simply turn the page and there, *there* would

be all the answers to what comes next.
To stand still is an adult thing to do.

What I really want is to run up and down
the long hall and make wild woman sounds.

Recent discussion on Heraclitus is that his
commitment to the flux doctrine and identity

of opposites results in an incoherent theory.
So here I am, back to standing very still.

# SLICKROCK MAZE

I wrote my cousin that I was climbing in and out
of a slickrock maze. For weeks now—no, months—
I've written these words: *slickrock maze.*
I hadn't thought about what it meant,

it was just words, then a heat wave hit
breaking all records. To a young couple
embarking on marriage, I phrased life
as a "slickrock maze."

All week we've had meteor showers,
swarms of earth tremors, high tides,
small-craft warnings. Northwest winds
are blowing up to twenty-five knots.

It's mid-August and the marine layer deepened today.
An upper-level low-pressure area hovers.
Clouds and fog cover the coastal waters.
It's 4:30 AM and the cats want out,

but I know the coyotes have been feasting
all night in the hills just beyond.
There isn't enough light to see the back fence
that leans over the ground since an earthquake

eight months ago. The cats and I sit at the window
and wait for first light—a sign
that will end a certain dislocation
from night—then, sweet Jesus,

light begins its spread across
the horizon, and a gray sky
is pitched perfectly for a slide deeper
into the slickrock maze of daily living.

# BLESS THIS HEAVENLY HOME

Our bell cow saunters into the lower pasture.
Somewhere nearby is a coyote den.

I hear them howl at night, though by then,
cows are all back in the barn.

I pad barefoot room to room,
each step assesses polished wood.

I think about that wood, warmth
and grain, as if each tree still lived.

I've grown as rooted as hill grass.
Every change in the weather is a gift.

Every prairie warbler, field sparrow,
grosbeak, towhee, dark-eyed junco

calls to me. Wind shifts through trees,
sings my name. I sit for hours, breathing.

I don't know when it began, but there is
no sound except rain and now soft light falls.

# CHILDREN, IN PRAISE OF

He sounded as if he was dying just
outside my bedroom window—
a blackbird, young,
almost as large as his mother.

She wanted him to hunt,
but he stubbornly refused—hunkered
down on a branch near her
wailing to be fed.

He was hungry, of this I was certain.
Nonetheless, he could fly,
had flown into the tree in my yard.
Now he faked his demise

with a performance so believable,
his mother looked uncertain.
"Horsefeathers," I said aloud,
"he's nothing more than a con artist."

She turned and looked at me.
"Horsefeathers," I said again, a little louder.
She flew off leaving the little bugger,
who immediately straightened himself

and flew after her.
He is who he is, I thought,
and feeling generous at the moment,
I forgave him as I forgave my daughter

the day I brought her home.
Even then, she had Sarah Bernhardt eyes—
that pinched, kissable mouth.

# NEIGHBORS

Half-asleep, I hear a dog barking.
I don't care what time it is.

I drift until my next-door neighbor screams,
*Shut that fucking dog up.*

If I'm right about the dog,
his owner is deaf as a stone.

I look at the clock; it says 3:58 AM.
The dog barks with more energy now.

My neighbor's front door slams,
rattling mirrored closet doors.

I make my way into the bathroom
and startle myself with the shag-nasty

looking back at me. Light from my neighbor's house
casts an eerie glow onto the pavement.

Only the man with the barking dog sleeps on.
He wakes at six, opens the sliders in his kitchen

after first grinding beans for his fresh-roasted coffee.
He'll call to his dog, *Here, Boy*—then says, *Good dog!*

as he walks through the side yard
with the dog at his heels and around to the front

where the man's paper will lie waiting.
The dog will dash ahead and pick up the paper

between his teeth. He will turn back to his master,
wag his tail proudly, then follow the man back inside,

where the dog will sleep his day away in preparation
for the night to come.

# DAYS OF HEAVEN

December clouds gather in the west.
The maples have almost finished yielding
their glorious crop of leaves to the wind.
Even squirrels seem to have taken
the onset of winter seriously,
and where they have stored supplies
for the days ahead
I know not, but know that…

I was thinking of something brilliant to say,
something that would sum it all up.
Words that a hundred years from now
someone would find written in an anthology
and know immediately what kind of day it was,
then the scampering of a squirrel across my roof
sends the cats and me to a window,
where I see the sky has cleared to blue.
Wind has come and gone, taking with it
what it needed from the day.
The cats see nothing that holds their interest
and tumble into a snarling ball
until I am forced to smack them
with an empty envelope.
Each day becomes more precious
than the last. There is no way to explain
such a thing.

## LIFE CYCLE

It is the beginning of autumn. I watch a maple leaf
blow across a sidewalk coming to rest before
being swirled to skip along helter-skelter. The leaf
is cured red and gold and brown and is larger

than a big man's hand. The tree, a sapling really,
aflame with color, committed to season.
Ah—daily now, the wind wrestles with leaves
and angel-wings them around our shoulders.

Summer lay under scorched ivy where a horse is buried.
Every year the ground sinks in a little more.
We dug the hole deep, had a crane lift our beloved
old horse into a pit stained by our tears.

We tossed in flowers—all we could find, so our
horse's nostrils would be filled with living fragrance.
We got down on hands and knees
to shove dirt over the edge and into the hole.

It took all our strength, we actually swam in the earth.
Not for a moment did any of us believe that our lives
would continue as before, that winter would come
and then spring, then summer. Not one of us believed

Benny Boy's death could have turned into a thing of splendor,
yet what I have told you is true. Even the sunken ground
is beautiful, like a bowl in the earth, or like the soil's inhaled
before it sings out the names of all 372 angels of death.

## DEATH, HOWEVER, IS A SPONGY WALL, IT IS A STICKY RIVER, IS NOTHING AT ALL
—Edna St. Vincent Millay

There may be snow before noon—
a front moves in across our pastureland.

Horses drift back to the barn. Cats huddle
over heat vents, dozing. A rabbit

is hunched beneath the porch. Thousands
of starlings have gathered in the upper

pasture. A snap of the fingers
and the flock rises as one, weaving

a polka-dot wave against the horizon.
I'm getting on with life, you see,

taking care of business. I've forgotten
all about my daughter, and all that came after.

Her lovely face, her hands, her car
that flew off the road into a canyon.

## I WILL TREASURE MY BREATH,
## I SHALL LINGER ON
### –Edna St. Vincent Millay

Days of sickness have tunneled into weeks, three weeks
of awful. Myself, yet not myself. A cold, but more.
The doctor's official diagnosis: *Something*.

So who am I to call it by a name other than the *Something*
it's already named? I've coughed so long,
the cough has become an entity, full of itself, demanding,

riotous even, breaking in on every conversation.
My cats simply look at the cough as a disturbance
that interferes with their naps. They curl into tighter balls,

hide their eyes with padded paws, and sigh.
My husband thinks it wise to escort this cough upstairs
to our guestroom at night. If I had it in me, I'd slit the throat

of *Something* and be done with it. Instead, I give it water,
gallons of water, hot soup, tea and honey,
little oblong suppressants. Still, it thrives!

Tonight the rain falls in earnest. I sit on the very edge
of our guestroom bed and peer out at a moon
that plays hide-and-seek with Earth.

Sometimes a constellation appears to bob to the surface,
then sinks again in rising waters. Stars blink on and off.
In the morning, I could drown in gratitude at still being alive.

## OH, THE SUFFERING—OH, THE PLEASURE

From a hotel window, seventh floor,
I see the Great Smoky Mountains.
Through glass, I hear the scream of a siren.
I take that back, many screaming sirens

race down Woodfin Street,
center of Asheville, North Carolina.
On the wall, a picture of a waterfall
hangs slightly off-kilter. Down the long

hallway to our room, the carpet is multi-
patterned, images tumbled to an end.
We eat breakfast in bed. I think of Nicolas Cage
in *City of Angels*, how he became mortal,

each sensation miraculous—taste, touch, sound.
And this morning, nothing hurts, nothing
demands attention, just the pure mortal gift
of complete awareness. Oh, the suffering,

oh, the pleasure—opposing realities.
We must know one to understand the other
a Taoist might point out. This me who sits in bed
holding a cup of hot coffee brought by someone else

asks why I would think of this in Asheville,
why not at home? But home has many demands.
Even leaving there was difficult—two sparrows
puffed up against a strong wind sat on a windowsill

in my library with cats but inches away,
a thin layers of glass separating the two.
Clearly, a picture of both sides of suffering
and pleasure.

## GRIEF: A GREAT SADNESS,
### ESPECIALLY AS A RESULT OF A DEATH
—(*Encarta Dictionary: English*)

A female cardinal flew into our glass door. She lies
on the deck, wings still and spread out.

Neck so obviously broken. There is nothing to be done.
The male sits in a river birch and looks

at the spot where she lies. He is magnificent in sorrow,
brilliant against the bareness of tree, fresh

fallen snow. We gently lift her, deliberate in our
grief. For three days after, the male appears,

expectant. The memory of her must sit in his mind as a thin
but measurable weight. It flies with him over

our steepled churches, the shingled rooftops, open fields,
the rolled bales of cut grass gathered for winter.

# THREE
## THE SCARCE SIDE OF MERCY

*"Finally, I decided that the proper strategy was to stare back."*

–John Green, from *The Fault in our Stars*

# REQUIEM FOR THE MARRIAGE OF MY PARENTS

She came from a time of the Great Depression,
my black-eyed, black-haired, swimming mother

with German stamped all over her name.
She met my blond, boxing father over a turkey's

slide from an oven onto the floor Thanksgiving Day.
His uniform impeccable, he'd sworn to protect

our country. I came along too late to save them
from themselves or years of pain. I would have

told them about the difficulties of separation,
changes our country would go through, how they

would learn to tear at each other, booze it up, fight
and lose. Oh, those beautiful people—so long dead,

I'd rewind them into life if I could, show them
the pitfalls, give them something to bargain with.

## CHEERS

All night I've waited for my head to stop pounding,
listened to the old grandfather clock strike off hours.
With first light, I think of Herb Summers and all
the other drunks I've known. I'm saying
two glasses of wine do me in, but I've watched Herb
lift a half-gallon of vodka to his lips, suck down
a significant amount, pour himself a stiff drink,
and stroll back to where the party was.

I watched my father pee in a closet, my mother
fall face-first into a plate of turkey and dressing.
I've witnessed these things since Jesus was a baby,
yet last night I lifted a crystal glass of blushing liquid,
inhaled its bouquet, made a toast to no one in particular,
and drank.

My father no longer looks for his glass eye
on a windowsill above his bed.
And I hope that Herb, the old reprobate,
has long since given up his need to sneak a drink.
I can't find it in me to blame my mother
for wanting to put a little zing
into her Tom and Jerry Thanksgiving morning.

It isn't true about last night, you know,
I wasn't alone, not really.
They were all there with me—hoisting their glasses,
all those serious drinkers.
I might as well say it, all those dead drunks.

# EARTHQUAKE

Finally one morning the house shook.
The earth heaved under us

east to west, west to east,
tossing dishes from kitchen cabinets.

Chairs and tables once rooted,
lifted anchor, shifted restlessly,

as if finding a new energy.
My parents and all their drunken faults,

clung to each other in a doorway.
I lay rigid in my bed

unaware anything different
was taking place.

## THINGS MY FATHER SAID

Lay that drop cloth flat, Kid.
Now pick it up in the middle
like you're making a tent. There now,
take your free hand and divide the cloth in half.
This takes two, Kid, remember that.
Painting goes better with a partner.

Burnt umber is your best color.
Never run out.
There—see it in my bag?
I always carry at least three tubes.
That's a painter's bag, Kid—
all those flecks of paint on that there bag,
well, that says this man is a painter.

Check out this wall, Kid.
Check it for holidays.
You know what a holiday is?
It's when you skip over a place
and it doesn't get painted.
Can't have no holidays now,
we're professionals.

Never put flat over enamel.
It will ball right up on you,
then you've got a hell of a mess.
Have to sand the whole damn thing down.
Check out what was done
before you come on the scene.
Some old guy could have used the wrong thing.
There are men like that out there, Kid—
don't know their ass from a hole in the ground.

T.S.P.—remember that,
cuts through any kind of grease.
I always carry some.
Look in my bag, Kid—see that box?
That's T.S.P.

Closets are hell—little rooms with no windows.
Give me the outdoors, Kid,
blue skies, a nice breeze;
small areas give me the heebie-jeebies.
A man starts thinking about a tall cool one
instead of his work here.

See, Kid, this here's a finish line,
just the right amount of paint
on the brush, but not enough to let it run.
Now, a steady hand, easy does it,
a perfect line.
Some old boys use all kinds of tricks,
but you might as well learn to do it right.
Be good at what you do, Kid.
Take pride.

And pay your bills.
Can't work if the paint store cuts you off.
Keep all the receipts too, so you know where you're at.

Clean those brushes good at the end of the day.
A man should take pleasure in cleaning his brushes.
A good brush, Kid, now, that's worth its weight in gold.
Clean 'um up, the way you clean up for Sunday school.
There now...leave 'um dry for the next day's work.
A good brush, Kid, is the painter's friend.
You take care of them, and they'll take care of you.

I know you're just a girl, Sis,
you're not growing up to be no painter,
but you don't have to be ignorant neither.
Show us some class now, Kid,
bring your old dad a beer, why don't you.

## MY SENTENCE

Every Saturday I'm sent to the movies with
one quarter: ten cents for admission,
fifteen cents for popcorn or candy.
I move between darkened rows,
feel the weight of heavy maroon drapery
as the screen becomes bigger than life.
This is where I learn how to walk,
what length a skirt should be,
and that having a man is the most important
part of any woman's life.

One Saturday I return home to find my mother
crying, taking curlers out of her hair,
arching her eyebrows,
dressing for my father
who called to tell her he has been released
from the detox center—
he is coming home.
She tells me how everything
is going to be different this time.

I watch as she brushes her hair,
blows her nose, and wipes at the mascara
smudged beneath her eyes.
Mother steps into a skirt,
walks to the mirror,
and giving a half-turn,
asks me if her skirt is too long.

# EMPTY DRAWERS

There was a certain kind of luck
when we stood in the kitchen
of that cold house with fire
in the belly of our stove.

We got dressed as quickly as possible,
huddled together sharing what heat
there was. If a fire was going
when I got out of bed, that was luck.

I'd run down the hall, down stairs
clutching my clothes, fast as possible.
If water wasn't frozen in our pipes,
how lucky we considered ourselves.

I don't remember my mother
being in the kitchen, not really,
what luck it would have been
to have that kind of mother.

Our cupboards stayed mostly empty,
their shelves supporting a couple of bowls,
cereal or soup. Once I got my own house,
I taught myself to cook. What luck,

to even live so long to reach an age
when I could leave. Fifty-odd years later,
all I have left of the place is a stunned
emptiness, sunlight through a window,

the day's sole sum of luck. A stove,
gray porcelain sink, dull and cold.
The days spinning out of control,
but I do remember believing in luck.

## STARGAZE

When I was six, Mother allowed me to choose
wallpaper for my bedroom. *Anything,*
she said, *any one you wish.*
I wasn't at all afraid of night.
I considered our celestial heavens
to be mine alone. Even then,
I preferred a night sky to daylight,
which I thought of as noise. I systematically
gave names to our constellations
before I learned they already had them.

It was easy to find north by way of Big Dipper
and Polaris. I knew by their brightness
which were planets, by their twinkling,
which were stars.

I stand at the window of my childhood home
looking out at a moon in Leo. It's a first-quarter moon,
delicate curve. I saw it about noon, and it's still here
at midnight. It comes through the window and makes
a ring of light where I stand. I hardly feel loss,
there is such joy in being here. This house is scheduled for
demolition in the morning. All who lived here are gone
save me—the single light
                              still burning.

# BLOSSOMING

I watched the sun come up, noticed a maple
just outside my window when movement caught my eye,
a California golden-eyed grass iris sprung open
from its pod. Overnight, literally hundreds
of tight-balled blossoms covered the plant.
I marveled at how I had walked past this plant
every day for the past two weeks
and had not once noticed it was flowering season.

Yesterday I got an e-mail from someone
I don't remember meeting who wrote that my poems
"went right to the heart, tearing through any barriers,"
and how I had "touched a space in her that had
never been touched." This morning my lover said
that I must have been made by angels.
There is so much to marvel over—
a perfect blue sky at 6 AM, cloudless even—
BobCat not waking me until 5 AM.
Last night I dreamt my father was in my kitchen
cooking potatoes and onions.

He had so loved waking the family this way.
I wonder how long it takes to come back
once you've died? Father has been dead thirty years.
Isn't it about time for him to make an appearance?
And my mother, she died on the same date
three years later. Isn't it about time for her to return?
I think I'll start paying attention to children.
I'll look into each little face for a sign of recognition.
I read someplace that before the age of four,
children remember their past lives.
I'd love to know they were back—a second chance,
taking in the trees and sky,
nourishing the world again by their presence.

# WHAT SURROUNDS US EXPLAINS US

Always at night, Mother would phone to tell me
I must tell my father he isn't to call her anymore.

She'd say, *I've had it with his drunken promises,*
and slur the word *drunken,* dropping the *p*

off *promises* so that it would come out *romises.*
Go to bed, Mom, I'll take care of it. Just get

some rest now. I'd start to replace the phone
in its cradle only to have it ring to life again

in my hand. *Hi, Kid,* my father would say, *ya need
to do somethin' for me, tell your mother I'm not*

*comin' ome— tell her now ta jus stop calling.*
I'll tell her, Dad, I promise. It's late now,

get some rest, Dad, and I need to get some sleep
too. *I know, Kid, I know. You're a good girl, all right—*

*it's how we raised ya. Take care of your mother
for me, take care of her. You only have one mother.*

# ANOTHER MORNING OF SUNLIGHT

Spring in San Francisco, I visit my father.
We rent a room-by-the-week near skid row,
a place where both of us can stay,
walk the streets together,

get Father out from sleeping in doorways
of those same streets, get some food
into him. But he got something in his eye—
his good eye, not the glass one

he'd take out at night, wash,
and put in his pocket like loose change.
He had to have some Visine, he said,
something to wash his eye,

something to take away the pain, his fear,
so he took my last twenty and left.
An hour later he was back with Visine
and a bottle of hooch. I don't know what kind,

I didn't know the names of alcohol back then,
all I knew was the bottle was half-empty
as his trembling fingers stripped off the shrink-
wrap on Visine. He washed his good eye

over and over until the liquor was gone.
He lay back on the bed with his good eye
closed, the empty socket of his other one
sunk in, Visine clutched in his fist.

The empty fifth lay on the floor beside his bed
in that strange room glistening in a morning
stream of dusty light that fell over a chair
where I slept, dreaming of nothing at all.

# FATHERS AND DAUGHTERS

The taxi pulls to the curb and stops where my father waits. Some say he waited an hour or more, though I was on time.

My father, he opens the car door, his hand immediate. His glance lowers to the toe of my shoe, follows the curve of my ankle to the sure round of calf, then continues the length of my thigh to that point where my skirt has risen, and continues to rise, as I pull myself free from the seat.

Love darkens his hazel eyes. My mother's ex-husband puts his arm around me. We have been absent from each other for two years. I suspect there have been women, but none that could know him better, know the flare of his temper, the warmth of his kiss on my cheek, his lap, the heat of his hand on my back, the timbre of his voice. These are mine.

"My dear, your legs are long like your mother's." This is not a compliment, but his observation, and I know there is no need to respond. I am grateful, for my mother is very beautiful. I bask in his approval. Is it not so that I have looked for him in every man I've known? Hasn't he told me I am his ideal woman? His image? I am his seed.

Inquiring about my life, he makes light of my dark comments and has much to say on the commonness of fragile relationships. His gaze is watchful at the curve of my throat. His eyes follow the rise and fall of my breasts. His expression becomes fierce as he acknowledges the glance of men who pass us on the street. This is San Francisco, the twenty-fourth year of my birth.

"My dear, you are very lovely. Men, they envy me. They wonder what an old man like myself is doing with such a young and beautiful woman. I see it in their eyes. They visualize themselves walking beside you, fantasize your arm looped through theirs."

He smiles at the wind gusting against my silk dress, how it flattens the fabric across my pelvis, binds it tight around my thighs. I listen to the tapping of my heels on the concrete, how I match his stride, step for step. He is solid beside me.

We do not speak of my mother again, or the distance that has grown between them since their divorce. There is no mention of other women. "Father, it has been too long since we have walked like this." My mother's ex-husband offers his arm. My fingers encircle his biceps. His fist presses close to his heart. I am no longer aware of people as they pass, or storefronts, or even the planet spinning on its axis.

# WINDOWS

My father reaches in the space
just above his chest.
Hand over hand
he pulls at some imaginary thing.

*Dad, what are you doing?*
I can't tell if he hears me
or if he even knows I'm here.

The days have grown long with cancer.
He continuously works the air,
adjusting, readjusting.

*Dad,* I ask again,
*what are you doing?*
He looks at me
for the first time in many days.

*Pulling the shade up*, he says,
*so I can leave this place.*

# 3:02 AM, APRIL, MY FATHER'S BIRTH MONTH

Three hours of agonizing struggle as we watch my father
climb death's ladder. Rung after rung, his arms reach

above his chest while his hands clench something
neither my mother nor I can see. There is an alarming stampede

outside the door, the whinny of rolling gurneys.
From deep within my father's chest, a full, round,

mechanical sound, his heartbeat registers on a screen.
So accustomed to this, I try to read subtext into what appears

in the steady, high-pitched beeps. How strange, yet gratifying
to watch these patterns repeat, knowing he is still here.

## LAST DANCE

Long before I'd thought about dying,
or lived with any understanding
death was an eventuality for us all,
my father said he wanted to be cremated.

He couldn't stand the thought of
being in some stinking hole,
eaten away by God only knows what,
when all his life he'd had itchy feet.

He was the kind of man, you see,
that needed to feel the earth
move under him, feel a warm breeze
blow though his hair.

He wanted that last chance to dance, he'd said,
on a hot bed of coals. Even dead,
he wanted his bones to jump around
until there was nothing left except ashes.

A social worker at San Francisco
General Hospital slides a standard form
in my direction. I can see Father's name
as it comes to rest in front of me.

A pen is placed crosswise on the paper.
The social worker's eyes are brown,
I notice, before she looks down
at her hands, one folding into the other.

A beam of dusty light falls sideways
and runs along grains in the wood.
Light catches the pen's silver clip,
refracting sunspots around the room.

I know signing my name, by controlling
the flow of ink that forms the letters
of my name, my name will be the last
signature on my father's dance card.

## MAGIC

Mother was always taking short naps.
*I'm so tired,* she'd say,
*I can hardly keep my eyes open.*
*I must find a place to rest my head.*

The family joked about her five-minute naps.
She would return even before we felt her gone,
laughing, ready for anything.
New Year's Eve morning:

Mother arrived for a party at 10 AM
wearing a rhinestone tiara.
She carried a sparkling wand.
*Magic!* she said, when I opened the door,
and rushed past/looking for something to bless.

Midnight: A whole year passes in this way,
friends kissing, Mother taking short naps.
We all sat down to watch television. *Times Square,* they said.

After Mother's gone,
after her ashes are scattered,
every time I close my eyes
a wand appears, the tiara too,
but no one brave enough to wear them.

No one left to bless us.

# HOW COLD THE NIGHT KEEN WITH HUNGER

Mother left for work at the usual time
wearing a dark orange jersey shirt
and slacks of rich, brown polyester.

She was in engineering, with privileged
parking, over by a fence where women
were escorted to their cars.

She worked swing shift at Hughes Aircraft,
Culver City, California. They were a team
and built the *Spruce Goose*.

This fence is important because at 2 AM
when their shifts ended, Mother and the others
met at the gate and were taken together

to that late-in-the-night, darkened
parking area. The other women told me
she said she was hungry, terribly,

terribly hungry, so one of her co-workers
fished three candy kisses from her handbag.
It was 2:11 AM. Exactly nine minutes

later, Mother parked her car at the side
of a road and police noted it there.
Three hours and fifty-two minutes later,

a second notation: Woman asleep—no warrants,
no previous arrests. Does not respond. A third
notation, 6:02 AM: *Waiting for coroner*.

# PASSING WITHOUT CENSURE

I knew instinctively as the telephone rang
it would be Mother—
drunk—looking for me to dole out punishment
so that she could sleep in absolution.
And, when I was unable to do so, made no comment,
she thought that I didn't understand,
that I didn't know she was drunk.
And she would tell me she was drinking again,
in fact, drunk—tell me
she was miserable beyond my comprehension.

The mortuary calls requesting fresh clothes
to cremate her in.
I tell them, *Let her sleep undisturbed.*
*When it's time, take her to the fire*
*unclothed and innocent*
*as the day she came into this world.*
*Exact neither punishment nor redress.*
*Let her pass without censure.*
I tell them, *Grant her absolution.*

# STANDING IN FRONT OF MARILYN MONROE'S CRYPT
## WESTWOOD, CALIFORNIA

Rosebushes are in bloom, heady red
and pink roses alive with prospect.

And always, there are fresh flowers
in a pewter vase attached on the left

of *her* marble crypt, the dying
flowers replaced twice a week,

dew of morning still visible
on each wilted petal.

Steadfast bushes are adorned with
bright buds, and below

thorns, past leaves, my mother's
ashes are scattered. People arrive

and reach out their fingertips
to touch Marilyn's final resting place.

Tears spill onto the ground and mix
with my mother's ashes,

and yes, she continues to force
even roses to grow.

# EARLY MORNING APPOINTMENT AT A FUNERAL HOME

First, there is consciousness. I open
my eyes to a darkened room.

In the distance, there is a muffled hum
from a car moving through the early hour,

slicing a lighted path on blacktop
wide enough for safe passage. The winding

road rises and falls off. My eyes open then close.
Something like terror has me reach

for my clothes, proper shoes. These feet have
educated me to their needs. They demand

and demand, and now I listen. Forget
transgressions, they will no longer be tolerated

and I turn on lamps until the whole house
becomes a beacon of light as rain falls

for the fourth day in a row.

# HANGING SHEETS ON A CLOTHESLINE

to blow dry

my mother rushes at me

  my mind

    God knows where

I put up my arms—put up my arms to defend

 against my mother's

    happiness to have found me

her unexpected kiss, touch

 my arms up to ward off and her tears

    tear at my heart-stopping defense

so unaccustomed were we

  to touch.

# BELATED VALENTINE'S
–for Michael

I am thinking about my brother this morning. He,
whom I haven't heard from in three weeks

must still be on that roof he said he was replacing
when the first in a series of great snows began to fall,

an uprising of snow grips the eastern states still—
twenty inches one day, sixteen the next, until the strongest

of roofs cave under that weight. My blood runs thick as slush
through this man's veins. I hold dear my memories of him,

first as a baby, then the smiling boy he grew to be. When he calls,
I concentrate on his voice, now the deep timbre of a man,

and I think of my great love for all that he was when he first
appeared out of the mysterious skirt of our mother.

## AT TWENTY-TWO

My daughter walks through life
in dresses cut so low,
her navel barely hides beneath.
These are the days of excess—
too much laughter,
too much red in her hair,
too much perfume,
really, just—too much.

We meet for lunch at a small cafe
but I can't get past her mouth too red.
When the hostess seats us,
a man my own age
follows her with his eyes.
He watches the sway of her hips
in four-inch-come-fuck-me heels.

When she was six, friends razzed me
about her provocative mannerisms,
a wantonness oozed from every pore.
They advised birth control pills in her cereal.
I have seen the way men adjust themselves
just looking at her. She is twenty-two,

and I want to lock her away,
wrap her slender body in white silks,
spoon-feed her warm milk and literature.
I want to rock her to sleep, kiss her
morning-fresh face—hold her on my lap again,
brush her long brown hair, and fill my nostrils
with her little-girl fragrance.

After lunch, we stand on the street corner
before saying goodbye. I hug her lightly
as I might a butterfly. I turn, wave,
and blow her a kiss.

# THE CEREMONY

I breakfast with my daughter who is getting married
in two weeks. We talk about flooding in Texas,
how it hasn't been this bad in years.
Two women at the next table talk about tidal waves.
My daughter's eyes fill with tears, and I ask
if she's feeling the landscape of her life changing.
I reach out and take her hand—I'm the mother,
after all, but I don't know what to say.
She tells me about wedding plans, how her future
husband will enter a medicine wheel

call for her by blowing into a conch shell.
She says she isn't sure how to answer—
maybe with a siren's scream—
maybe just by entering the wheel like a cloud
in her long white gown.
For the life of me, I don't know what to tell her.
I don't want to think of her life being as difficult
as mine, or say how grave reality is in the dailiness
of living. I can't say anything, for all that I don't know
sits on the tip of my tongue, and I can't remember
what it is I need to say.

## MY DAUGHTER

Well, I've called her that since she was six,
said to me, *Mother, a man came to the door*
*after you left this morning.*
*He called your name, but I didn't answer.*

She is naked when she tells me this.
Bending over at the waist
as she wraps a towel around her head
and folds the two halves into each other,
then twists them together.

My daughter is tall.
Her breasts are small with darkened nipples.
At twenty-eight, she is slim as a child.
I continue to stand in the doorway watching her
as she steps into the shower.

I am thinking of that other thing
she told me earlier—about her grandfather,
her father's father,
how when she was fourteen
he held her by the arm so tight,
and drooling, called her by her grandmother's name.
"Dessie, Dessie," he'd said, and left a dark,
wet circle on her blouse
over her breast
before she could push herself free.

Later that same day, she told me,
he showed her
in the Bible
where it is written
that women are unclean
when they bleed each month.

## NO HEART CAN BE HIDDEN IN THE GROUND

Daydreams are a form of reality,
someone once told me,
a separate dimension

where fiction and fact
blend like eggs and sugar
beaten into a sunny concoction,

grainy in substance
with sticky qualities.
Maybe it was my daughter

as she whipped heavy cream by hand,
or rolled a lemon-pepper pasta
she hand crafted and cut

into wide strips, then served
with a drizzle of extra-virgin olive oil.
I breathe in this scene,

dream about calling family to the table
where we will sit and wait
for the door from her kitchen to open.

She will appear wearing my red-checked apron
to offer her latest creation.
I can't tell anyone about this dream.

I don't even want to think
about the accident,
that cliff, the valley below.

From her kitchen, some sweet melody
I won't recognize
will float around the dining room—

so different from the rhythmic beat
beat      beat      of one lone drummer
where many gather

and together, slowly, enter the garden
to scatter her ashes
    among vibrant roses.

## IT IS SOMETIMES NECESSARY TO WEIGH
## THE COST OF PLEASURE CAREFULLY

That raggedy old mockingbird
is back. Thank you, God. He's taken up
in a tree across the street instead

of his usual hangout, our pine,
with its limbs brushing along
the bedroom windowsill.

And just because we've had two days
of sunshine, that bird has confused
blue of sky with spring, love,

and the blooming of flowers.
Last night, in candlelight,
my husband and I cradled glasses

of wine when we heard an earthquake
coming, one sharp jolt of ground.
There was only time to set our glasses

on a table. Each day brings
a new mystery. I can't blame
that raggedy old bird. Hope

beats strong in his chest. Today opens
to rain, and I'm thinking any minute
the earth could swallow us whole.

# SEPTEMBER CAN BE THE VERY BEST MONTH

On that hill above the pasture,
a barely visible pinpoint of light.
Too early for the bell cow

to have left the barn. I am in the South
now, no more boring California coast
to deal with, no ships queuing up

to enter port, no Sunday drivers with
car tops folded neatly inside their trunks,
no trash pickers coming around at 5 AM,

no bass hammering the air from boom boxes
or car radios—especially no wind blowing sand
in my face every morning, every night—no familiar

streets, no lawn blowers, no traffic jams, just that
pinpoint of light on the hill above the pasture.
Now I hear the bell cow's clanking as she leaves the barn.

## WILD CIVILITY

A warbler so yellow came to sit
in a young Leland cypress

and sang the soul of his tremendous
heart out. His song twice the force

of other birds much larger.
The sun rose to stand directly

over our heads and a soft wind
fluttered around our shoulders.

Pollen filled the air of a fine spring,
and everything was good. Our grown

children popped in and out of a sunny
doorway to the patio with steaming dishes

for breakfast and we were happy, truly so.
By 2 PM everyone had departed, traveling

to separate parts of different states.
I was alone. Clouds blew in. Rain assaulted

the land and by morning, snow. Into my
great solitude, the precious warbler returned

once again. It is enough for now,
the quiet of snow, the company of a warbler.

## PERVERSE AND FOOLISH OFT I STRAYED
—Henry William Baker, 1821-1877

The spruce forms droplets of rainwater
on every needle. Nine doves hunch

together under splayed branches. I open
a window and a pair of yellow finches fly

into a river birch. It isn't cold exactly,
just wet, very wet after days of a steady

downpour. Why, I haven't seen stars
or the moon of hope for eleven days now,

but rather many shades of gray.
Isn't that just a perfect metaphor for life!

What bothers me most about today is I could
stay in bed, stretch myself across the bed,

or let my head rest at the foot. I could curl up
on the floor, for all the world cares. It's all

shades of gray, right? But, no, I get myself
up, talk to my husband, who reminds me

how comfortable *he* is on the *other* coast.
There are many shades of sin and guilt,

self-pity surely being one. I'll go to church,
ask for and receive forgiveness. I order

a pizza and eat half of the darn thing—
that's something to beg and grovel over.

## ALONE WITH CHILDREN

Alex on my lap, her cap of swirling
dark curls mussed, yet perfect somehow.
Quiet at last, her tiny body damp,

she leans into me, holds my finger
while Darrian, not quite one, negotiates
his way around the coffee table,

staggers around the side, then
a controlled drop to crawl three feet
to where his pacifier lies—*Binky*,

his parents call it—
and while speaking in tongues,
he crawls back to the table

by means of which he hauls himself
upright. Walking, really walking now,
he comes to us, arms outstretched,

offering a gift to Alex, his *Binky*,
doing what he can too, so concerned,
to comfort and console too.

# WHEN GRANDCHILDREN COME

Playing grandmother this weekend,
doing what grandmothers do,
the nine-month-old pulls herself up,

high-stepping to and from
next step, then another, surfing,
her mother calls it, a developmental milestone.

I cook, straighten, smile a lot,
happy with the hubbub
of my husband's daughter, their family,

baby Maggie, red hair, hazel eyes,
lifting her arms in wild enthusiasm.
I love it all, every moment,

and what I love most is
watching Julie, my husband's
fourth daughter of five, the wild one,

mountain climber, triathlon competitor,
the one that dyed her hair green as a teen,
who took a bus to Canada with $10 in her pocket,

found a place to live, job, boyfriend, all in a day,
this woman with a master's degree
teaching her baby sign language because she can,

now motherhood and enjoying every second
of baby Maggie. That's what I missed,
so busy working to make everything just so,

I missed the joy of each moment
each milestone, every first, just being.
That's what I learned, a milestone, even now.

# AFTER A THOUSAND TRAGEDIES

Wind moves through our trees.
A hard rain last night left the morning sky
gray, grasslands green. Buffalo prevail,
as if anchored to ground.

We've brought an air mattress, and like children,
we run from room to room, finally settle
in the master bedroom that only faintly
smells of paint and varnished floor.

Its interior arch perfectly frames a wide-paddled
fan. The blades slowly, methodically stir
heavy air. Legends of the South tell of
gracious living, no one here seems to hurry.

Life took our pasts apart, steered us
to this unfamiliar country, this state.
We built this house of stone and brick.
The windows and doorframes persist,

as bricks soldier around each opening and along
the foundation. As if to make us all whole, defend.
It's time for chaos and loss to make friends.
It's time to make this our last stand.

## REALITY

I watched a movie yesterday, broad daylight,
a movie I'd seen before, twice even,
with no interruptions—well, a cat wanted in my lap,
jumped down, then wanted back up and down again,
that sort of thing, but those aren't interruptions,
that's just normal. Now, watching a movie
in the afternoon, even if it is a Saturday, truly that is
worthy of note, when in a few weeks I'll be leaving
this place we've called home for the past five years,
there is yet so much planning and packing ahead.

I do love a good movie—think of it, to live someone
else's life for an hour and forty-three minutes, experience
where they are and where they've come from,
acting so believable, it makes me catch my breath
to walk in their skin and when it ends, the final credits roll,
it leaves us beaten up, but alive and isn't that just like life?

# FOUR
## I'M TELLING YOU, I WAS READY FOR ANYTHING

> "I cannot make you understand. I cannot make anyone understand what is happening inside me. I cannot even explain it to myself."
>
> — Franz Kafka,
> *The Metamorphosis*

## MAPPING NAIL MOONS

June, sweet sixteen, leaning
against my mother's Olds, Don Fowler at my side,

ten years older, with
blue-black hair, looking directly into

a Brownie Hawkeye that took black and white
images of what was then. I was so in love—
this was before I knew what love was,
knew anything of how it worked.

Sixteen, and the scent of him, his aftershave,
even the way his shirt collar wrapped around his neck,

sent me into living a dream, wondering what kind
of wedding band, white dress, and steepled church.

Oh yes, his tanned arms, slender hands, his fine-boned
tapering fingers, squared nails, white moons, those moons.

A close study should have informed
my sixteen-year-old heart, pressed hard

against the cavity of my chest, falling in love
was the easy part—the hard part always comes after.

## BITS OF FLYING GLASS
   –for Elizabeth

At last we realize there's no one
but ourselves to sweeten
a torrent of days, stacked
one against the other,
with no proper bookends

to keep them together. Our souls
just erupt from our chests
as we turn, bent on facing
into the wind. See how easy
it is to get all worked up

just sitting, maybe looking
out a window
at someone you swear
you loved
only last week?

Better to gather eel grass
or ostrich eggs than to slide
through that cave of despair
you just happened upon
while holding a book

about some far-off place,
wondering too, what clothes to pack
for that quick getaway from the death
of a relationship, while you're singing
a breathless song about love and release.

## RED CORVETTE

We streak
through the canyon,
a blur of red
in my husband's
convertible.
Even strapped in
I feel precarious.

My husband says,
"*When you die,
how do you wish
to be disposed of
after you're gone?*"
And I, accustomed
to acquiescence,
ponder what might
be reasonable,
consider what
it might mean
to be without
human form.

I say, *I'll give
it some thought.
It's an interesting
question.* I say,
*I'll think about it.*

Hunkering down
in the seat, I pull a scarf
from my purse,
cover my head,
tighten the seat belt,
and turn my face
to the sun. Yes, that—
the sun on my face—
my hands—
feel—the wind sting.

# NORTH ON THE 101

Sunday morning—we head north into vast, unfettered skies.
Simon and Garfunkel sing "Homeward Bound,"
an omen, I think, as we snake down the Conejo Gradebetween neat rows
of lettuce and squashand glimpses of the sea, pea green and calm.

The off-ramp at Camarillo State Mental Hospital
looks inviting somehow. Just for a minute
I think about asking my husband to stop, ask him
to let me rest. Oh, not forever, you understand,
just long enough for some quiet time,

maybe a meal of fresh garden vegetables
brought by an angel of mercy
dressed in soothing white, a nice contrast
to this vein throbbing purple at my temple.
I watch as houses hug the coastline—holding on for dear life.

I pretend I don't see oil derricks,
offshore drilling—for God's sake.
Sometimes I wonder if I'll ever really live.
I mean, utterly give myself over to feeling things hard
the way others seem to.

I've never completely participated in life, you know,
not with my whole heart at any rate.
Think of Tess crawling into bed beside Ray
after he'd gone. Needing to hold him one last time,
*brush lips to know an ending*, she wrote.

Loving him so much,
even death couldn't rob them of intimacy.
No, I've never loved like that.
I haven't lived enough
to have loved like that.

## LISTEN, PLEASE LISTEN

I lie down for a nap, but every time I close my eyes,
whitecaps heave the bed around.

I've forgotten the feeling of safety in his arms.
The night is quiet, a sleeping volcano.

The phone rings twice, then nothing.
Lately, I've been looking in a magnifying glass.

Listen, please listen.

The sky flashes electric: *SEX  SEX  SEX  SEX.*
My hands are numb and I have grit in my teeth.

I'm building walls again,
we haven't made love in months.

Left lane, left ventricular, left hand,
left brain, nothing is right tonight.

It's Tuesday—he just turns on the television.
Now I cry only on odd-numbered days.

I can't imagine Christmas coming.

# COME, SLEEP! O SLEEP, THE CERTAIN KNOT OF PEACE
—Sir Philip Sidney

Fourth floor, private elevator,
plate glass windows with a view
from breakwater to Earth's
far curvature. Cats draped

on wide window ledges, ducking
when seagulls fly past at eye level.
Imagine          such luxuriousness.

Dolphins swim back and forth,
mild temperatures and sunshine,
sunshine galore.    *Wintering,*
we call these months here,

away from home. Sleeping late,
long beach walks, lots of fresh
produce. None of that old life

hanging around    empty bottles,
alone for days on end, bills
accumulating on a table.

All I had to do was leave the bum,
kick him to the curb                move,
start life from scratch, lose everything
to begin again at fifty-something. Imagine—

# MY NAME IS STELLASUE

Which means star and violet
as though a deep purple of longing
is a narrow band of light
that spreads unto its own spectrum.

Blue-white I burn
for the cool touch of a man
to still the vagrant ghost
of loneliness at midnight.

Hear the wind?
Quickly, quickly it gathers
kindness spilled in sleep
no other world can offer.

I sparkle with heaven's grace,
feel the weight of winter's approach,
a silence and gentle gloom of years.
Deep in the blue well of my eyes

lives a raggedy child-spirit
whose voice awakened is a variable star,
bone by bone, breath by breath,
named perfect

in my imperfections—
transcendent of plain face,
breasts, sloping shoulders—
ablaze with consuming desire.

## LACE AND THINGS

Where this drifted in from, I've no idea,
but my thought started right after I hand-
washed a silk blouse, and dripping,
hung it to dry in a morning breeze,

about this half-slip,
lace flowing from the hips down,
pure white, Glenn Davis IV
gave me when I was just sixteen.

It came in a plain box with a dozen layers
of soft white tissue that made a rustling sound.
Peeling back the layers revealed an exquisite
lace thing, handmade, and delicate to the touch.

Now, thirty-five years later, silk blouse waving
in air, droplets of water falling cold on my face,
I remember that lace thing, buried still
under other lace things, not nearly as delicious.

# GIFTS FOR THE MOON

Tonight, gauze covers the face of the moon,
almost to obscurity—so I want to say something
kind for the moon—with its barren valleys,
dusty molten rocks: I pick forget-me-nots
for you, moon. I understand loneliness.

This is March. In the heavens you journey
even as I am stationary. Captured by this room
of wood and glass, that one ambiguous star,
my bones have become meteor-like, more
luminous and incandescent.

Were a lover here, I could long for rain,
the split crash of knotting thunder dazzling
our ears. Deep in the bruised rhythm of his blood
rushing through his veins,
I could touch an index finger to his wrist

without waking him, breathe when he breathes,
raise new latitudes of wanting. I can do that!
And the curved shell of his ear might wonder
at the impulse spiraling him upward into consciousness,
might wander through zenith heavens and

forked lightning to break free at last
from the clustered images keeping him company
in sleep to find me quite near.
See—from the twisted rain leveling the ground,
rainbows arch.

# PATTERNING THE EDGE OF REASON

The admission begins with pressure,
his thigh resting briefly against the back of her thigh,
his breath passing over her shoulder
to circulate between her breasts.
Then there is the brightness of the room,
the darkness of need,

a room—filled with people milling about.
O how the moon struggles to rise.
A low-frequency hum wakens the synapses.
A thousand pulses a second
race two hundred miles per hour,
routed from one neuron to the next.

They reach their target in the brain—
the trunk of a tree manifests as man,
a wild root.
Desire becomes that—
moisture seeps through cracks and crevices
rising from the ground organically.

The matter of the thigh again,
and the groin—a separation.
We live in this place:
the windlessness of a full moon,
sounds of the Pacific Ocean in our ears,
then a long curve, and back-curving into bare reality.

This is the trunk of man: struggle and need and
memory. Cathedral bells ring in a forgotten night,
ripened melons and body fluids, rain dreams
patterning the edge of reason, an admission
of possibilities, a direction everything is headed.

# I TOLD HIM MY NAME WAS AMELIA

Yet passage from one day to another,
we stand transfixed as broken weathervanes,
rooted inescapably in our longing to spin;
how that which is hidden
becomes that which we desire most.
We strain against the patterned fabric of our lives.

Then—the night gets flayed before us:
I told him my name was Amelia,
shrouding myself in mystery
so that desire would become a bright flung thing
shimmering in frivolous light.
The sky of crimson floats like tattered silk—

O moon of yellow-jacketed faithfulness,
I beg to lean against your fat forgetfulness,
stand in your glow, your pure, bright-ridden valleys.
Go ahead, cobblestone my heart.
I submit to the incandescent midnight.
In truth, we all swing between intimacy and isolation.

I'll stretch out and trace a long-forgotten
incision along the belly of hope as if it is a highway
taking me someplace I've always wanted to go.
We are carved so fragile, we transcend the mundane.
Soon enough our bodies will be rushed into graves.
Soon enough nothing begets nothing.

# DISMISSAL

Under the humidity of September,
my body heat rises from bed
and is caught in an overhead fan.
It whirls around the room.
Things insist on remaining displaced

as a moon high in the sky after dawn.
All memory of night I left in a ditch
along with candy wrappers and clots of dirt.
Rain dried as it hit ground leaving not a trace.
Picture me: a drunken sleepwalker

suspended between feathery slumber
and a harsh, falsely lit way station,
mad from heat and rain and an ethereal moon.
Real life seduces, then dismisses,
and no one stands on a platform to wave goodbye.

What chimney-sooted heart of a louse
with only stolen hours to give
sheds promises with such solemn gravity
before sun rises to guile the day silly?
I need to tell you these things:

Dried rain leaves no odor—
compulsion expands year after year
until you become only more
of what you've always been,
until even faith is extinguished.

And yes, the moon is still there at noon,
and yes, at midnight,
when the sky is bruised black
with your longing.

# TEMPERATURE

Men have called from both coasts, men who,
like the hundred monkey theory,
have grown concerned about me:
husbands of friends, ex-employers,
men I've known since college,
men I've just met, they all express concern.
Several have used the word *horny*
and though I know what this means,
each night I run my hands along my own smooth
skin looking for hardening, permanent structures
that might have started, but find nothing unusual.

One of these men on a trip to this coast,
took my hand and pulled me onto his lap,
whispered in my ear his desire to be of service.
Another hugged me to him until my breasts
were pushed flat against his chest,
my thighs pressed against his own.
One kissed me,
exploring the inside of my mouth with his tongue,
yet my teeth remained cavity free.

Perhaps I should be concerned about myself.
Oh, I've heard about women like me,
divorced women—living alone.
Maybe it's my poems—
the red lingerie I wrote about.
I admit a few have mentioned this,
loosening the top button on my blouse,
sliding a finger along my collarbone
to touch the red silk bra strap.
I want to assure everyone I'm fine.
My God, screech owls mating in the top of trees
hardly disturb me at all.

# JAPANESE APRICOTS BLOOM

They can't keep their hands off each other—hands, arms,
lips, chest to chest, they hug, gazing into each other's eyes.

The courtyard is surrounded with Japanese apricots in bloom.
Under an overhang, a railing made from rounded steel pipes

forms a fence. The young man lifts his petite prize and settles
her on a bar, then wiggles his body between her legs.

She wraps her arms behind his head, runs her fingers
through his hair and bends to meet his upturned face.

They don't seem to notice the man walking his dog,
or me, just a few feet away, coffee steaming

from a cup cradled between my hands. I lift the cup
to my lips, *my* lips, with their own voracious appetite,

pursed to blow a cooling breath over the top of that dark,
pungent liquid that must, for the moment, satisfy

my longing, as an afternoon sky fills with blackened
clouds and drops the first rain of another fall.

# MEXICO

Quite near, a ringing bell awakens me,
and for a moment, I pretend I'm in a village,

perhaps Mexico, a street just off the plaza,
alone in a small, comfortable room

painted the color of sky without clouds
or vapor trails. Off to the north

is a jagged mountain range
purpled by atmosphere, gladdened

by twisted trees that fill with wind
so their canopies sway. A melancholy

overtakes me knowing none of this is true,
that I am in a world of my own making.

Oh, the blueness of sky is real, my gown
of spun green silk gathers around me

and flows out onto white sheets, all real enough.
The day always starts before anyone is ready.

The truth is, I am alone. The thing about the bell,
that is real, I can hear it clearly even now

through mist of morning, and it reminds me
of a village in Mexico.

# AIRPORT

The lounge area for incoming flights has a Starbucks,
a few easy chairs, some straight-backed chairs. A man

sits to my right, leans backward on two legs of a chair.
He holds a cell phone next to his ear, and speaks softly.

I hear the timbre of his voice as he asks a question,
then listens. A light shines overhead as a spotlight.

Deep shadows cast from the light's trajectory
make his eyes appear sunken. He listens without

change in facial expression. He listens and then
brings the chair to stand on all four legs.

The heel of his right foot taps the airport carpet twice.
A tear escapes the misty spring of his left eye

and becomes a sheer filament coursing down his cheek.
He taps his heel again and with his free hand

spreads moisture evenly across the roughness of his cheek.
He listens, bent forward, while I look anyplace but at him.

# REPORT

I read it in the newspaper:
a woman—naked,
covered in blood,
was seen walking
the old Townsgate section
of Westlake.
Police were called,
but when they arrived
she had disappeared.

I tell you this now, it was me:
stripped bare, bloodied,
I walked from my marriage.
That was last winter.
My footprints were quickly shrouded
with brightly colored leaves
of orange and gold.
This is California, after all;
a sun without ending
devours the years.

## GATHERING

Early, Anne and I walk the hills
and watch for a red-tailed hawk
usually perched in one of the tall pines
crisscrossing the back road along a creek.
We pick dandelions and chicory for tea,
clusters of wild mustard for salads.
The sun falls hot across the canyon
giving permission to a choir
of ragtag-manic blackbirds
in search of insects, small fruits, and seeds.
I tell Anne I want to marry again—
want to fall asleep curled in the arms of a man—
wake wrapped in body heat
two generate during a stone-cold night.

Late, near the end of a poetry reading,
I turn to see the head and shoulders of a man
with his back to me.
He leans into a table,
intent on what is being said.
He must feel my gaze, for he turns
and looks directly at me.
I say nothing, but grow hot to near cracking
as a seed might from a tall pine
before bursting into new life.
He sits back in his chair—
gathering the heat.

# CLARET OR TEA

It's morning. I know it's morning because my cat sits just to the right of my head watching for a sign, any sign, I'm coming into myself. I feel her breath on my cheek. Although I'm sure I haven't moved, she starts purring. I open my eyes and she is where I knew she would be—so I get up. I fill her bowl with Savory Salmon, replenish the kibble, and wash the water bowl before filling it too, with bottled water.

For myself, I make a cup of coffee and open the back door. I take the coffee and a handful of submissions out to the steps. For a few minutes, I just sit with my back against the door listening to crows having a morning discussion. After things grow quiet, I listen to wind blowing through eucalyptus trees and squirrels chasing about.

My neighbor opens her back door and steps out with a watering can. She looks delighted to see me. I am wearing only a T-shirt and panties. It doesn't matter, I think, I could be wearing army fatigues and she'd find fault.

"Say," she says, in a heavy Italian accent, "aren't you chilly? You should put on a pair of sweats. Are you walking this morning? It's a holiday, you know. Where is your cat? I haven't seen that man you've been dating. Aren't you seeing him anymore—what's his name? Aren't you friends with his daughter? What does she think about the two of you not seeing each other anymore? And how's her husband now that he's home from that hospital where drunks go?"

"Morning, Delia." I say, "It's a glorious morning."

I pick up my cup and the submissions and return into my house. I walk to the furthermost room, away from the back door. I read a poem about a woman who is visited by another woman, a strange woman, who wears a Panama hat and no makeup. This woman with the hat asks her hostess what she plans on doing with the rest of her life, and the hostess, knowing some questions left to themselves, answer themselves, asks her guest if she would like claret or tea.

I put the poem down, take a long sip of coffee and think, "Why, since Delia moved in, I've hardly had to think for myself at all."

I pull on a pair of sweats and go for a walk. When I return, I look for my cat.

I find her sleeping. This job of standing watch until I've come into myself must be exhausting.

I call the daughter of the man I'm no longer seeing and ask about her life, her husband. She tells me that everything is fine, really fine, and she thanks me for calling. She says that it's good of me to remember her.

"Oh," I say, "I was reminded of you just this morning."

Returning the phone to its cradle, I wonder if things might have turned out differently if I'd had the courage—yes, courage and something else, I'm not sure what, if I'd had what it took to have my drunken husband picked up and taken to a hospital. Would things have been fine, really fine for us?

I read another submission written by a man. He writes about feeling trapped in a suburban cul-de-sac by burglar alarms, doors, and windows that have been double locked. He grieves over kingdoms his Phi Beta Kappa key can't open.

I take off my sweats and make another cup of coffee. The cat comes to oversee my activities in the kitchen. Wind rattles the back door.

In a while, I'll return to bed and sleep. I'll dream that someone claiming to love me calls my name over and over and over again, but I don't have what it takes to force my mouth open and answer.

# MOVEMENT OF STILL LIFE

First Saturday Art Walk, streets jammed with artists
and art lovers. We park next to a gallery,

open the car door into a stunned reverberation,
something flying through air, a ribbon,

maybe sixty feet wide and, this is hard to judge,
maybe a mile long. *What is it*, I ask, as we join

a group standing in the heat of night looking up,
wine glasses in hand. The gallery owner tells me

they are Brazilian bats, and I ask how she knows.
She repeats the saga of one flying into her gallery

a night two weeks before. We watch as wave upon
wave swirls in air, bats squealing, wings agonizing

the dark. Inside, a leggy blue-eyed blond has created
a body of work, perhaps fifty charcoals and pastels—

heavy paper stretched over inset frames to simulate
canvases. Inside each, gray rooms hold dozens of round

tables, straight-backed chairs, windows and doorways
backlit, in an unidentified light source of old gold.

Each room devoid of life, abandoned to time, dustless,
yet lifelike, as if one could enter. The rooms hold

their collective breath. If any spirit lives inside,
I feel none. It also seems possible to step through

paper into any one of the rooms, exhaling to add
movement. A door into the gallery opens, air shifts.

Bats crisscross a gibbous moon, screaming,
as their wings batter the air.

## ON VIEWING A TURN-OF-THE-CENTURY
## DOLLHOUSE STAIRCASE

I'm hard at work here—controlling
the muscles in my face into a forced, relaxed,
noncommittal expression. My hands
hang listless at my side without inclination
or impetus to any exertion. Upon inventory,
I catch my head tilted to one side and quickly
right it, face forward, impartial
and without biases.

The subject is a photograph: A beam of dusty
light falls down a staircase. The man,
the woman, as if having fallen from heaven
unclothed and open mouthed in passion,
cast shadows forming an extension
that could or could not be measured in
the present tense—and I am thinking
of how dry my own mouth gets, the dark

cavern that creates a round sound as it escapes
into a candlelit night—a black moan.
And, Eve, Adam too, all through the ages
the crumbling facade of need. How do we
manage a single day? The pain,
excruciating loss, tragedies stacked
one upon the other as my own hand
rises unconsciously to brush a tear
that rushes wildly down my cheek.

## SIGHTED

Everything sleeps.
Still, I'm not alone.
See how night deepens
all around me?
Stars light blackened skies
and blink at each corner.

I know the moon is huge,
like the body of Christ.
My lips shape His name,
pray—each step I take
I count as my arms reach
through emptiness.

I see I've come naked and long
into this world. I've lain in the stain
of seasons, felt them hot
against my thighs.
My street was lonely, each door
and window an entry.

Tomorrow I will hold the day fast
against my forehead.
In the thickness of my throat,
I have felt an onset of madness.
The red pulp of my lips
will not form a sound.

# SOMETIME BEFORE LIGHT BEGAN TO FADE

Hundreds of irises rise up.
Over winter, they have divided
so that a field of purple appears.

This land also remembers
when it grew scallions. Each
year a few long green leaves

wave about, just because they can.
Many new calves populate
the pasture, and our own leopard-

spotted Appaloosa we named
Wind Rider, grows more each day
into the joy of her name.

Still, there is some dark spirit
just outside my vision
as I walk through a forest

of river birches to a tributary.
I sense its heavy presences.
Clearly my life is privileged.

My body remains whole, my mind
intact, at least as intact as
it has ever been, yet there it is,

that dark spot between trees.
Something I don't want to understand
waits there. I can feel it stomping

its feet more each year, biding
its time, licking its lips in anticipation,
even a slight panting.

## THIS DAY

I've lost track of the date—
it's somewhere in the middle of June,
but the exact date is a mystery to me.
My friend Robert once told me

he went to Hawaii for a weekend
and ended up staying five years.
He came back to the mainland
when he lost track of the year.

I know the year, the month,
and decided to stay home today.
I left once, only to walk over to the post office box.
There wasn't much—a shocking telephone bill,

a letter from my ex-husband saying
his sorrow over our divorce
*grips him like the earth grips her dead.*
Well....

I watched television for an hour—
a movie about a woman someone was trying to kill.
*We are all dying of something*, wrote Donald Hall,
*but our degree of awareness differs.*

What difference the date—the year,
each morning the sun swabs the canyon in light.
Goldenrod covers grassy slopes.
At midnight, pine-scented moonlight

streams through my bedroom windows.
I sleep naked and long,
concerning myself not in the least
with the passage of time.

## WITHOUT LOOKING BACK

She exits a taxi and without
looking back, enters a moving sidewalk
that takes her toward a waiting plane.

Reaching *terra firma*, she steps up
into the cabin of the jet that will
carry her to a city deliciously unfamiliar.

In the time it takes to get there,
she will reinvent herself, change her
lipstick from soft mauve to *Firecracker Red,*

wrap a perfumed scarf around her shoulders,
something light and carefree, that might
flutter in the breeze of a late afternoon.

She will seek out her assigned seat, read
numbers posted below the overhead
compartments until *her* number appears.

It will be then she sees the man, already seated,
smile, and when he looks up to meet her gaze,
she will notice his mouth gape slightly

as he unsnaps his seat belt, moves quickly
to uncurl himself from the confining space.
She will step back, let him enter the aisle

before she takes her place at the window.
Already her new life has begun. No longer
secretary, or teacher, or receptionist,

but a new person she creates, an identity
for a woman who wears *Firecracker Red* lipstick
and exudes a fragrance known as *Interlude.*

## YOU HAVE TO KNOW

*You have to know what's more than enough to know what's enough.*
   –William Blake

He arrived at the museum
seconds late, in a hurry, his long legs
propelling him up the worn stairs
two at a time. How could he know
*she* was all he had thought about wanting,

that he would be her everything, and
the luck of it all, both of them having more
than they could possibly stand of the others,
to know exactly what it took to be enough.

## CONCERNING LOVE THEN

If a man has the spirit of his youth
and hasn't become hardened,
and as well, has the courage
to love a woman in her sixties
as he might have when she was thirty—

well, if I were that woman,
I'd wake each morning
having found something to cheer about,
maybe the sound of rain on a roof
or an ordinary owl hooting.

This, of course, would add color to my cheeks
and a glow of expectancy
about just how bright the future of a day could turn.

Then should you be here for a visit,
I would tell you it happened just today—
morning sky still darkened,
a rain-slick street unfettered,
and every curve of my physical structure
molded to that man's body, wrapped
within his arms. I'd tell you at last
I understand he isn't going to let go,
that it is reasonable even, to find love
as whole and perfect as light
falling across an eastern sky.

# HOW TO HOLD YOUR ARMS WHEN YOU'RE IN LOVE

Time wants to show me a different country.
It says that North and South can join

and take away separation. So that one man,
one woman can live in a place both call home.

Home is wherever *they* are. Family will become
the common denominator, and time will allow this gift

in a million different ways. I have saved for this day,
tucked my love away in the museums and churches

of my heart knowing one day a love that can endure
for all time would step forth. This is the way I hold my arms

when I'm in love, outstretched, palms up, sending all the light
I can manufacture to learn our natures and become one.

# THE KEY, MY BREAST, THE MOON

Here is a key to my house.
Think of it as afternoon light
poured liquid over our bodies.
What remains is a willingness
for communion, mingled with hunger,
ignited by fire, and pounded into the shape
of a rugged trail that leads to my door.

Until now, there has been nothing of value kept here.
Think of this key as an uncharted pathway,
study the multifaceted leaves of the arroyo
willow from my bed. Watch how beveled
glass allows leaves to spiral in wind. Imagine
the leaf hairless—without intention.

The door of my house is concave,
hollowed inward like the curve between my breast
and my stomach that allows light to pass through
and the moon to rise from the sea
to that point just above this house.
We will re-landscape—that rugged trail
leading to the door will no longer be needed.

Let it return to its original woodland of interior live oaks,
shrubs of monkeyflowers and manzanitas—
the great horned owls might return.
I tell you this—after two days and two nights
the world outside will no longer exist.
This key I hand to you will become a band of gold.
Let it encircle your finger.

Let it weigh light on your tongue
as a communion wafer.
Here is the key—
take it.

# HEAT

I slip into a pair of blue Liz Claiborne shorts
as if it was just any other afternoon.

Later, he slides his two hands down
my hips and shorts fall around my ankles
where I step out to slow dance
around a table to nothing more than the hum
of mosquitoes buzzing against screens
on a breathless summer's eve.

Sweet Mercy, I am thirsty for the salt in his skin.
I run my tongue along the gulf of his collarbone
and can't remember who I am.
I kiss the curve of his spine
and find a path that leads me on.

Mapped out, my life looked like an arid region.
This man understands an arroyo.
Together we are water,
each crevice a safe harbor on another continent.
We are pulled down by gravity
in a dark tangle of mouth and limbs.
There is no way of separating
where I end and he begins.

## JAMES BOND BEACH

There is nothing unusual about the day—
the sky takes on light about 5:10,
I turn the heat on,
feed cats, nothing I haven't done
a hundred times over.
No—a thousand times,
maybe even a million times by now—
who among us figures these things out?
Yet last night,
last night I was in Jamaica
walking along James Bond Beach
in the buff.
Honey, in Jamaica, waterfalls cascade off hills
right into the sea.
Why, trees grow right out of the surf.
It didn't matter to me that I was naked.
I'm telling you—I was ready for anything.

## DO IT

When flirting, look directly into the eyes of a man
as if needing to tell him something.
Turn the palm of your left hand out,
curling your fingers slightly.

Stand still—as if lost for a moment.
When accepting a drink from your hostess,
take a sip and imagine him unbuttoning
the fourteen buttons at the back of your dress,

how his forefinger and thumb work,
each disengagement granting permission.
Feel warmth from his breath in your hair.
Pause! Understand the space you occupy,

the timbre of wood,
tempered glass.
When he speaks, listen.
Touch his sleeve and concentrate

on the craggy lines that form
around his mouth—the feathered wings
sweeping up from his eyes.
If he touches you,

arch your back slightly,
then bend one knee.
Your hips will sway.
Lift your left arm

and touch the back of your curled fingers
to your cheek.
Bring that arm to rest against your breast
applying pressure. Be willing.

When dancing, be fluid in his arms,
dreamy, like floating,
the music hushed like sea water in your ears.
When it ends

do not step away too quickly.
Stay another moment
as if you are recording
the first grain of sand

on the first beach.
Tremble without his heat.
Don't speak,
but promise him everything

with your eyes.
When he takes your hand
follow him into midnight.
You—woman—

with your head full of swarming gnats
and your senseless curled fingers
crazy from want.
Take what you need.

Do it!

## ADMISSION

There's that moon again, February moon,
moon in Aquarius, Valentine's moon.

My mind is wrapped around a possibility
others seem to have found a whole lot easier

to comprehend than I, this Valentine's Day
thing,              this love thing,   that

*one man for the rest of your life*    stuff, this is what
I'm talking about. Now I have that man, and he has me.

All I can tell you, dear reader,      silly-happy, crazy-sad,
angry enough to think about doing all kinds of evil,

he still holds me and I,
by some stumbling grace,        allow it.

# AH, MEN

And now, along comes a man
who sends a perfectly sensible woman like me
browsing through lingerie catalogs—
things satin and lace,
exquisitely shaped chemises
with lavish lace bodices—
or here,
a sheer stretch body stocking
with embroidered patterns
of bows and wild geraniums
all in black.
I think about a hard rain,
answering his call in a red dress,
pressing my body against his solid frame.
If only time would advance slowly
as his fingers lift the hem of my dress—
luxurious red satin panties cut thigh high,
matching red embroidered bra,
beautiful scalloped lace molding the rise and fall of my breasts—
I would capture his breath,
hold hostage his mouth.
My kiss would sit on his lips like a scarlet flower,
and the rain,
a virtual wash of filtered light
scattering fluted designs filigreeing everywhere
for a perfectly sensible woman like me.

# SOUTH ON I-65, TAKE THE LEWISBURG PIKE TURNOFF

My husband is away and although I had
been looking forward to restoring order

in the house and finding a new home for his
miscellaneous piles of papers and magazines,

now I find it unnerving to live in sure neatness.
He calls to inform me he is in Fort Smith, Arkansas,

and tells me tomorrow he'll reach his destination.
The cats don't like his absence, and I'm sure

I don't either. He says he has sighted a ghost town
off the highway, and although he searches,

he can't find a road that will take him there.
It is very clear to me that without him, there is

no home. With him gone, *we* are a ghost town.
I text him the directions to home.

*Forget the ghost town, I say,*
*we are alive and waiting for you to return.*

## YET WHATEVER IT IS WE SEE IS HARDLY THERE

Just before he left for a month,
my husband hung a picture

40 x 60 of a hallway
in striking shades of yellow

and a banister, blurred as if in motion.
Light streaks through an open

window, plays across my bare legs,
warms the skin on my arms.

His picture is huge on the wall.
It becomes a pathway into another room

and because it's near a window,
I imagine where this hallway might lead.

He is a Photoshop Jedi, a master of all things.
A magician who can make rocks dance,

banisters move, a moon rise full, stars shine
in broad daylight. He can erase the mist of dawn.

# DAILY SPECIAL

Birds start to sing. They inform me
the hopeful work of rain is done.

Though others might call it wild talk,
I say these winged scribes announce

a whole world has been righted. Overhead
thunder still resounds, but these birds

continue their morning proclamations.
It is a joy to see the mud-splattered earth

rich with rivulets from a downpour.
Where I grew up, rain was a scattered

affair, a morning wind that carried mostly
empty promises. I would bake sweet morsels

to remember the day. Today's sweetness
came over the phone, my husband's voice

from 2,200 miles away. He sang
a few notes from a song in French

which reminded me all manner of gifts
can bring warmth to an open heart.

## BLUE SKY

High above pedestrian streets, I think
of myself in a tower, as the Virgin Maiden.

Sirens scream far below. In my imagination,
they become alligators in a moat.

Determined wind comes from the north,
pushes at clouds. Morning and evening

skies are red waves spilling
across twenty-foot-high windows—

walls of steel beams and thick glass,
man's idea of strength and style.

Mother told us red skies meant Santa Claus
was baking cookies. I remember many ways

she tried to make us secure with mythic
storytelling—money in the proverbial cookie jar,

guardian angels, saviors from every religion
watched over us. No opportunity,

no chance for wrongdoing—a sky full of birds
kept us from harm. Big and very bad

people lived in the world, this we knew.
There were plenty of old women

who lived in gingerbread houses,
ovens large enough to hold my brother and me.

Today, a black cat follows me from room to room.
Sunlight fills every recessed corner,

while from somewhere, music, ethereal, angels sing.
North pushes all clouds aside.

# SKOL

Plenty, more than plenty, has been said about love—
but dinner tonight finds us sitting in

front of clear Lucite mats, placed on a glass table that fits
so perfectly in our bay window.

Freshly mowed grounds with roses blooming all around.
On our plates, arugula turned

gently with freshly slivered garlic cloves, olive oil,
sea salt, served with two thinly sliced

pieces of pot roast, wine, grapes, almonds. My foot
resting at ease against my husband's leg.

He lifts his glass to make a toast—*To all the soft, sweet
days of our life together, my dear.*

## WHEN THE MOON AND SUN
## ARE ON OPPOSITE SIDES OF EARTH

Cross the bridge over Kennedy Creek and you might see
a great blue heron in flight, his wingspan at least six feet.

He follows the tributary that runs behind the old Methodist
church—the one that sits on cinder blocks. Two years ago

when I first arrived in Spring Hill, I would have thought this
scene astonishing, yet today, the heron and creek are as much

a part of me as air that flows oxygen into my blood supply.
Green populates my world: pastures, trees. Blue defines

the edges: sky, water. Each day my husband and I treasure
the warmth of our home, our gibbous natures now blending,

red in every room, bright and hot as our love. A yellow waxing
moon rises, greater than half but on its way to being full.

# LETTER TO ERIC

So many books, hundreds really, my very own
personal library of poetry. It's poetry that saved me.
When I think I can't think about what comes next
after so much went wrong, I remember the luck

of finding love now, and too, the kind of love
Valentine's Day was created for, a day for lovers.
That's what I'm talking about. Today, Valentine's Day,
February 14. We've sold our home. The escrow is flying

through without a hitch. We made an offer
on another house in a different city. It's all poetry,
you know, my days, certainly nights, it's these books—
poems keep on writing themselves in my head.

When I was young, I remember being happy
or sad, but I couldn't just be. Poetry has taught
me that, and how to love. So this is a Valentine's letter
to my husband. Our being together

has made my heart safe. You, my darling,
are the subject of this poem. If I didn't
have poetry in my soul, there would be no poem
and no reason to write this letter.

## NEED DID NOT WAKE ME

 nor fog, cold, or anything that has so often
taken away my sleep before. It was a dream in which I,
an observer, watched my husband as a boy of nine or ten,
walk along a path beside his father, a tall man, though not as tall
as his son would become. The father had broad shoulders
and something just right in his vigorous step, allowed sunlight
to bounce off the deep waves in his hair.

Since I am the one on my back,
a comforter drawn up around my shoulders,
I can tell you it is possible to step from that wooded trail,
hunting rifles put neatly away, to picture my husband,
now a grown man, surrounded by his five grown daughters
and a warm fire, aglow with light as all of us laugh
from the sheer love of being together.

I left our bed, left my husband sleeping, to sit by that same fireplace.
I gazed through French doors out into the garden and followed
a path of roses, pink, red, yellow, white, lavender, and gold.
*How is it possible*, I thought, *to have roses actually gold?*
The girls all have their own dear husbands now,
children to care for, they are off in their dreams.
I hear my husband move about in the bedroom.
He'll soon make our tea. When did the day begin?
Where does the dream end?

## LATE JUNE

Dawn Sunday, and the cat yowls at the back door,
then lunges at it, as if by doing so
it will open magically.
I roll over, eye the clock: 5:16 AM.
In the bathroom, I remember a dream,
children in car-boats, laughing
in the cool waters of a lake.
The mirror reflects a woman I hardly recognize,
tousled hair, china-blue eyes, a bright spot on each cheek,
breasts, high and full, and the skin around the nipples
light, as if dusted with powder.

I am living on the brink, I think,
as if my whole life stretched before me.
*Abracadabra*, I say to the woman in the mirror,
and push my arms through a T-shirt.
*Open sesame*, I say, and pull on a pair of shorts.
Magic, and the coffeemaker clicks on.
This is how I start the day,
start another year,
start the rest of my life,
relentlessly—as morning turns the sky crimson.

# WINTER SOLSTICE

Under a chandelier at the front door
of a retirement home, I walked into a four-way
cane fight over a prissy woman,

all pink frills and bubble-gum lipstick,
senseless as a chicken, still able to cause
a cockfight and leave a trail of yesterday's perfume.

At the core of us, it's always about sex.
Small children, babies even, know from birth
how to flirty flirt. It turns into the tug of pigtail,

twirl of skirt, all at the root of it, sex.
Boys learn the macho walk-walk,
girls go for the plunge of a neckline.

It's all about sex. You've heard loose change
jangle, caught that sparkle of earring,
and you know generations to come are assured.

We are all like winter hornets
soldiering through four-dimensional space
looking for a place to die.

# FIVE
## DARK LEDGE OF NIGHT

*"When everything seems to be going against you, remember that the airplane takes off against the wind, not with it."*

—Henry Ford

## DRINKING FROM HADES' MANY RIVERS

We drink from the river of Lethe to forget.
Some ancient Greeks believed that souls
who sought reincarnation had to swallow
river water so they wouldn't remember.

It doesn't matter what, let's just call it life—
that which flows from the headwaters
located in this earthly paradise, found
at the top of the mountain in Purgatory.

In the short time it has taken to write this,
the marina has shrouded up in fog. Imagine!
Fogged in and forgetful. I have to ask the question:

*Where do I fit into this outrageous life?*

## MY ALEXANDRIA

The house is coming down.
The house is coming down,
and our architect says
once the bulldozer starts,
it will come crashing down with
shocking speed, a pile of rubble
within an hour, guaranteed.

Each night I dream I'm homeless.
Each time more disoriented, utterly
insecure. The rain, a whitewash
that blocks all view of my garden.
I've already been told to make friends
with the idea the plants will go too,
all turned to rubble during construction.

Tonight I will think of Tess
crawling into bed with Ray.
*Kiss lips to know an ending,*
she said. I will lay my head on my
own pillow, perhaps weep a little
while the windows are all open
and an overhead fan whirls.

Tonight I will draw this house around me,
this not-so-safe haven, and meditate on
the sorrows of Alexandria, how the lighthouse
stood even after many earthquakes until a fort
was built using its fallen stone.

## SUNLIGHT BRIGHT AS HEAVEN

Delia wakes to sunshine streaming around the shade,
*like an eclipse*, she thinks, and slides from bed

without disturbing even air. She puts on her work
clothes, goes out into bright light to plant sunflowers,

six of them, one for her husband and five
others. Her *men,* she calls them, two named

for her brothers, two for her sons, and the last for her
father, dead these many years. She pats the soil

at the base of each tenderly, brings a hose around
to give them a wet start. *Light will do the rest*, she says.

She fixes a nice breakfast before going to wake
her husband. *Get up, you sleepyhead*, she says,

lifting blinds, one by one. Sunlight falls
through dust particles rotating soft as other worlds.

She takes in the complete stillness of the room,
calls his name, but knows he is already past answering.

Each morning, she waters her sunflowers, and by summer,
her *men,* are eight feet tall. During the day, each follows the sun.

At sunrise, they face east as Delia walks among them, cooing.
Delia looks up into their flowering heads and pours out her love.

She tells them of another world she will soon enter. She tells
them to be strong. They listen and continue their rotation to light.

## LIFE AS A BHIKKHUNI

To live by *that* set of rules: meditation,
prayer, if you'd rather. I can tell you,

it's an introvert's dream. Think of it,
just to sit and observe every detail

of a pink scale gayfeather sunflower,
similar to a sharp gayfeather, but with

long, linear grass-like leaves, loosely
at right angles to the stem—who among us

has that kind of time and all the while
work is right there in front of us,

calling our name. Work—meditation,
two opposites. To find such bliss

one has to be somewhere not here,
somewhere tropical, not where the low

is 18° like it is tonight. So bliss has to be
not in a place, or in things, or even work.

No, the bliss we look for is hidden within,
the last place any of us think to look.

# DESPITE A LOT OF HIGH-PROFILE PLANNING
## AND A GREAT DEAL OF MONEY

the house had become unmanageable,
its packed boxes stuffed into every corner
but I hadn't touched the books, not yet—

they would be packed last, each box
exactly 16 x 16 x 12, the volumes
themselves so variable in height,

width, and content. Alphabetically
was the only possible way to file them
if I hoped to find any one of them again.

Only the must-haves would earn space
on the new shelves and too, books tended
to multiply as month after month

after month they spill out their
lies about clumsy living,
failures and fate, and facts,

don't forget facts, not to exclude
their sad deprivations,
now unburdened.

# NO WAY HAS YET BEEN INVENTED TO SAY GOODBYE

I'd flown Burbank/Las Vegas, Las Vegas/Burbank.
It was late, and I was tired.
Rather than join the rush to exit,
I stay in my seat and watch the ground crew

clear out the underbelly of the plane.
I don't have any luggage,
just a new book of poems by Jim Harrison,
the one dedicated to his brother's child,

dead at fifteen. Gloria     Gloria.
I watch a canvas bag with a big red heart
sewn on its side bump along, throbbing it seems.
Finally, the stewardess comes for me,

has to remind me it's time to leave,
time for the cleaning crew to come aboard.
The captain and co-pilot follow me
down the ramp. I turn the corridor in time

to see the two men link arms and whistle
different tunes, shuffle sideways.
Somewhere, someone claps.
I am quick to weep.

The days have been back-to-back clouds,
my spirit broken as easily as a wishbone.
Gloria          Gloria          Gloria.
I used to have a gun in the house.

It wasn't the cold black of the thing
that frightened me, it was me,
fear of what I might do. I held its coldness
to my forehead once, hoping to freeze the fire inside.

I think she must have drowned. Jim never says,
but much of the book is about water.
Last night I had this dream: I was swimming
at the bottom of the sea, so alone, it's deadly.

## FINDING NORTH

I can't find a room far enough away
from either voice or train.

Day after long day, there is no
solitude, no time to think:

computer, phone, music
from cars on the street below.

No dew-fresh morning walk
among trees that all day listen

to wind. North, they say, is where
wisdom can be found.

# LOST AS A HUNTER HOME FROM THE HILL

My husband, lost with his camera on friends'
150-acre farm, stumbles upon

an old barn leaning into the earth,
a fallen tree, deer at rest in a meadow

and a small herd of goats guarded by a fierce dog.
Eric appears out of the woods, an apparition

with a bloody knee. He seems oblivious
to the damage, and looks in wonder

at the wound, wipes off blood with the back
of his hand and asks for a glass of water.

All the next day he spends in his studio. At nightfall,
he emerges with his knee bandaged

and three museum-quality prints. An old barn,
there since the beginning of time, goats,

their ghostly forms woven among tall grass,
and deer, in peace before hunting season.

# AFTER A FIVE-HUNDRED-YEAR FLOOD

I am alone out on Carl Road sandwiched between
Spring Hill and Leiper's Fork. I park on an overpass,

roll windows down for a better look at a tributary
to the Harpeth River watershed. It curves south.

Water is deep and flows around a tree, surely
a thousand years old, it has grown so large,

it's deeply rooted in the riverbed. Dogwoods
whisper, *Rain, maybe tomorrow, early,*

*while you sleep naked and warm*
*with your husband beside you.*

Only an occasional snap of a twig startles damp air.
How odd to think it was just last week this road was

washed out, evidenced by weeds caught on a fence
five feet high. Debris hangs like so much laundry to dry.

# VIEW FROM INSIDE OUT

Their lives are all sunrises, walls of glass,
and great smugness. When they visit

people in houses with windows that allow
only a small part of outside vastness in,

they return to their sixth floor loft of steel,
grateful for glass panels floor to ceiling.

Yet over breakfast they talk about moving,
words sliding off slick-surfaced glass into air,

and just to back it up, they spend the day
on their computers, no more than twenty feet apart,

looking at small houses with tiny windows.
All day windows appear on their screens.

What they find, they email to one another.
She likes them oblong, he likes them square.

All day and into sunrise of the next morning,
they talk about making their world smaller.

# ONE NIGHT IN THE LIFE OF A POET

All night I conjure up slicing a pie—
how each slice becomes the name of a poem,
like in a table of contents.
I wake, think this thing over,
then drop off again only to see the pie.
How clever I am to have thought this up,
worried though, there might not be enough
pie to go around.

Morning, and I can't imagine what any of it means.
Why it was important—I can't remember the flavor,
or know for sure if I ever knew.
Later in the day, I pass a stack of books on the floor
piled one on top of the other.
These are books I want to read as soon as possible.
The stack is six-foot-three.

Later, I buy two more books and a stepstool
so I won't fall adding the books to my stack.
Soon I'll have to move to a new house,
one with higher ceilings, it seems.
Night brings a meteor shower. Stars fall
an average of thirty-seven miles a minute.
At midnight, I take a blanket to the yard and wait
for hours, watching for anything to move.

# I PRAY FOR COMFORT TO A HOWLING WIND

Dark recognizes only its own dark self
on nights like these. I pour a glass of wine
while gathering up Raymond Carver books.

In the cold gloom, coyotes bark
at the edge of our property.
I hear their pups yipping to be fed.

When we were young, my brother and I
plodded along, Cheerios for breakfast,
baloney sandwiches for lunch.

Dinner could be another bowl of cereal
or a plate of nothing. I lived in a state
of frightened loneliness in which

so much depended on my reaching maturity
while my parents rushed in their frenzy
toward death. Ray Carver would understand.

He knew fear and loneliness. He escaped
into his beloved fishing. I buried myself in books.
Tonight I bridge the distance between us,

Ray in that other world,
me in this breathless, brutal darkness
of what we call *life*.

## SLEEPING

3 AM, alone! This is an oxymoron—alone,
here in the canyon as I am, working from here.
However, even now I'm not entirely alone,
a truck has passed the front gate four times.
It moves slowly, with emergency lights blinking.
Three manuscripts wait to be read.
Cats want to be fed. Bills need to be paid.
So I get out of bed as chimes announce 3 AM.
There are forty-eight books in my office waiting
for their chance to shine. I imagine them
ruffling their pages, creating a stir.
The telephone comes to life—someone looking for Jose,
but when I tell them Jose isn't here,
they call me a liar and hang up.
The phone again;
screaming this time, liar—liar—liar—liar.
The cry seems to startle the 4 o'clock chimes.
Cats return to their beds. Coffee is gone.
The books seem to have given up,
as have the manuscripts and bills.
The street is quiet again; however, the truck, I see,
is now parked across the street.
I can just make out the writing on a side panel—
**Jose— Housepainter.**
What amazes me is yesterday was Easter Sunday
and I didn't know until late in the afternoon
when a neighbor called to invite me to dinner.
Maybe if I turn out the lights, pull the covers up
under my chin, maybe I can sleep a little—
not the deep restful sleep of an innocent,
but a few minutes here and there.
It all adds up, I think,
it has to all add up to something.

# TUTORIAL OF PRACTICAL INFORMATION

From the balcony, a great blue heron is in trouble
with a pair of gulls. From my vantage point,
high above the water, they appear to take themselves
with great seriousness. Their bodies fully extended,
wings flap madly in air, and I can't help
but feel sorry for the great blue. He's looking up,
defensive, in his effort to protect himself.

Halyards clank against mains.
Water laps at the sides of boats.
So much drama, and the sun not yet in sight.

A life vest so small, a child hardly old enough
to feed itself must have let it drop into
the sparkly waves to see if it would float.
It does and becomes my morning present.
A sign, perhaps, a new day, a beginning,
fresh start to an old script—all regrets gone,
the longing too, as well as this child's,
all of it. I imagine him still in his little vest,

still kicking his darling baby feet,
his piggly-wiggly toes magnified by water,
his plump mother's milk-fed arms flailing, even
his shrieks of delight or fear or frustration—
take your pick. There it is, all balled up
into one great heave to crush my heart.

By noon, the vest is gone from view.
The tide goes out, and I am alone.
Come back to beginnings, back to a fresh start.
It's all the body knows, all one can do.

# MORNING IN LONG BEACH

California, after an absence of not quite a year.
Between buildings and six blocks from the ocean,
alleys shelter many homeless.

Buses squeal to a halt. Starbucks everywhere,
like churches in the Bible Belt. Sirens scream,
citizens run for shade and shadows to evade

a fierce sun. A woman breastfeeds her
newborn while two street people discuss
which way to go, west to the water,

or east. *No telling how far*, one of them says.
A pigeon gives up searching for wayward
crumbs and awaits their decision.

*Let's check for butts first*, says the tall one
and shuffles toward a bin. Morning glories grow
along a wall and up a telephone pole.

California! I haven't thought about this state
for 359 days—site of my childhood,
place of my parents' deaths.

## SWEET DISORDER OF DRESS
   —for Drude Clark

I watch the waves roll toward shore,
curl one way, then another, always testing.

I've dressed in yesterday's clothes as if today
was an extension of what's already happened.

The cats must have picked up the scent of Raven's Call,
a place where rushing water and peaceful spirits

roam freely among oaks and sycamores.
Each cat studies a muddied shoe while I cut open

a sweet lime grown to please the gods
and squeeze its juices into my hot tea.

# NEW YORK, NEW YORK

Everything this morning is about New York!
A phone call from my husband who is in NY
for eight days. He's enjoying the weather.

I got an email from my high school historian,
a classmate died yesterday. She lived in NY.
Trump defends rape charges. He's from NY.

The rest of the news really isn't news at all,
just people acting like escapees from
a local loony bin. It is all just so New York.

A literary journal comes by mail with a tribute
to NY writers. They write about Central Park,
Poe Cottage, a room at the Marriott Marquis,

Times Square, Woodhaven in South Queens.
I'm to have dinner with a friend tonight.
She just returned from, yep, you got it,

New York. The stars must be aligned—
Nashville nonstop to New York.
I shut my eyes and a plane appears.

## ASK ME

Ask me in a hundred years,
I'll remember the wind,
boats off shore rounding the fourth marker,
cumulus cloud buildup due south
and along the foothills.

I'll tell you how the same people passed by
two and three times while I read, while I
looked past bright umbrellas,
looked out over water
to the blue curvature of Earth.

Everyone has experienced waiting—
first, impatience, a wrestling that goes on
inside the mind, this fact, that fact,
the *what ifs.* They can't be ignored.
No one can help with this, not really.

I don't intend to hear people's conversations,
words that set my mind churning, like *Shhhhh,*
which means nothing at all, though it's an order.
And I wonder about people—a man with his
pregnant wife sits scowling. He's handsome

and stares past infinity, oblivious to all. His wife
rocks their one-year-old. I wait, my hair tossed
by wind, pink spreading across my nose. Hours
with nothing but time to think what it is
I've been so obsessed with all my life.

## UNWELCOMED ADDITION

It isn't clear to me if Blue Ridge, Georgia, is in the Great Smokies.
It is in the mountains and somewhat hazy outside, so—

Looking through the window, I see an old flatbed trailer.
I'm surprised I came up with this term "flatbed,"

not because I know it had someone asked, but because
it was there, in my mind, pushing past all the other useless

information I once had and feel has receded, as a pond recedes
between long periods of little rain. Sumac grows behind

this flatbed. It has turned bright red. It's mid-October,
Sunday, early. Light softens the cheap and dingy motel room

where all I think about is getting out of here, and wondering too,
at the real possibility of carrying away a bedbug or ten.

## MONTEREY

It has stopped raining. That's a start at any rate.
Even in bed I'm cold. I know what it means
when people say *cold to the bone.*

The bone in my foot aches, the one I broke
years ago. Even in a knee-chest position,
even with a heavy winter coat on top of covers,

I am cold to the bone. And this house—this house
is saturated to the point it droops. Windows are swollen,
doors have to be forced open and closed.

I pull on the warmest clothes I can find,
a heavy polo sweatshirt with a hood.
Its cheerful red seems out of place.

Hoping for some comfort, I take a winding
path down to the sea. Wind is punishing.
Gulls circle overhead.

A cormorant dives headfirst into water.
No muss, no fuss, a clean, easy kill.
A lone fisherman appears

and sets up on the sand. He smiles,
I smile. It's a reflex action.
Back at the house, my friend

should be waking. It will be her
first day home from the hospital.
It's near the end, they say, near the end.

## ON THE SOUND

Here on the Sound, the Strait, they call it,
whitecaps toss about. It's rough,
and a couple of small boats are still out there
making a run for safety.

Earlier today, I took a walk in the woods.
Wind was high in the evergreens,
it roughed me up pretty good.
My God, I was lonely,

I could have been the last person on Earth.
I walked to the graveyard for some comfort,
then kept on walking into town.
I rubbed elbows with strangers,

sipped a cup of brew at the coffee house,
bought a huge bouquet of flowers.
I walked so far those flowers were half-dead
by the time I got them into water,

wind dogging my every step.
I think it might rain tonight.
One of those storms without thunder would be nice.
I'll light a fire—keep the flames alive.

I'll leave all lights in the house burning.
I'll talk with rattling windows and wait for the sun
to come up—wait for the sun to break
from the dark ledge of night.

# VIEW OF THE WORLD FROM A HOTEL PATIO

Thomas Wolfe's home is across the street,
place of his childhood, where stories exploded

in his mind like Molotov cocktails. An impressive
house, yellow, no lights burn within.

A structure rebuilt to hold Wolfe's accomplishments.
A hotel stands facing the house, a nice hotel.

I have a room here, guaranteed for two nights.
The light is diminishing in Asheville, and it's raining.

Leaves on surrounding trees drip with excessive
moisture. No matter, the patio is covered

by a glass overhang. *Ah, is this not
happiness*, said Li Po. Or was it Tu Fu?

# DEERFLY WISDOM

A deerfly hovers near my eye. It inspects
me pore by pore. I swing my arm in a broad gesture,
and it follows, riding on my energy. I need to tell you
I thought to clap the thing between my hands,

send it to its afterlife, but it never stops its scrutiny
of me, and in time I come to feel accepted,
adored even. Before me, redwoods cover
an entire mountainside. Eyes closed, I allow

what surely must be a wisdom of sorts to pervade
my mind. It tells me to be true to myself—
just like that, to be present to each pore in my body,
offer no resistance to change, be flexible in this day

of conflicting times. In the presence of tall trees,
something opaque appears to drift groundward,
I won't tell anyone lest it make no sense. I allow
all my childish dreams of mercy to float the Earth.

## TRIP

Take a child who just wants to know
how a leg moves in its hip socket,
or what makes the ocean stay in one place
instead of running flat over all the land.

Now, let's say this child grows up,
lives a crazy life, grows old—maybe grows mean,
like old Mrs. Harrington who lives up the street.
One day the neighbors realize no one has seen her

in a long time—weeks in fact. People gather
out front of her house. Everyone puts in their
two-cent's worth as to what should be done.
Meanwhile, days earlier, the poor old soul

just settled down on the front room sofa,
covered up with a blue-and-white checkered afghan,
and drifted off to sleep wondering if there is a Saint Peter,
and if angels have wings, when out of her dream,

a white light appeared and a tunnel.
She might have remembered reading
about reincarnation and left us then,
wondering too, if it could all be true.

# GARBAGE

Dusk—trash is put curbside to wait through the night.
Boxes UPS delivered, empty now, fruit and juice containers

Costco packed with our purchases for safe travel, and trash,
used paper, coffee grounds, just trash, wait through darkness.

Three men wind along our country roads to gather these goods,
happy to see what waits in both perfect and imperfect order.

People wave from porches, return the men's smiles
and sometimes talk for a moment, as their big truck idles

patiently, waiting to resume. We never think about our discards,
ever; that's for these men, with their bright, intelligent faces,

who take charge of all we don't want. We entrust them with our
refuse, our garbage, and with gratitude, we wave them on their way.

## UNSEEN, YET I HEAR THEIR QUIET DELIGHT

In this garden, gifts given *in memoriam*,
a lawn chair I sit in even now reminds me

that Tooty and Jimmy Bradford gave this
for Winn Robertson and Will Parry.

These people hardly sound real, but Cheekwood
in April with its dogwoods in bloom, and tulips

of every breathtaking color, is most
certainly tangible in every respect.

I give myself over to breathing, watch
the soft rise and fall of my chest. Here,

on the hill overlooking three ponds
of flowing water that make up this part

of Cheekwood's Japanese garden,
I distinguish nine different birdcalls.

Cumulus clouds move south to northeast.
I think they are the souls of all these people.

Even for those remembered, the work must
continue to separate their past from some future.

These heavy-winged dear ones, awake
or sleeping, they that death has taken,

only I keep their names present.
Each moment *in memoriam*.

## SHAKY GROUND

How meddlesome the wind,
narrowing to steal beneath the door,
sneak between the louvers.

A distant cloud is blown up
to thunder us silly
and has sent the stars scurrying.

The bare maples tremble
with each stab of light,
every boom to another stab of light.

Leaves scatter and thrash about.
A white birch kneels,
her spindly arms frantic in the air.

When a knock arrives at the door,
I imagine it to be the postman,
imagine inviting him in,

fixing tea, perhaps—
when I open the door,
wind rushes past

to ransack the room
before finding a place to settle.
I fix tea

and frown upon my solitude.
How I've cultivated a quietness of room
and grown unsettled as the weather.

# ENVIRONMENTAL PORTRAIT

At midnight, I retire to the whine and boom of
Roman candles as it rains color across the sky.

July heat requires little in the way of covers.
Youngsters are tucked into their own safe beds.

At dawn, smoke lingers in the damp air.
Finch fledglings sit on a bird feeder,

flutter new wings practicing an ancient
ritual of piercing chirps, when translated,

means *feed me*. It has been hot. Even the rabbit
is in poor humor. I place my hand inside

my own blouse to find a heartbeat. It continues
in steady rhythm, still hopeful, although

beginning to sense an end. After all,
fall of the Roman Empire was nothing

more than a complex transformation.
Outside, life is abundant.

# OUTSIDE ROOM 104A
### *Do Not Resuscitate*

I find the light best sitting in front
of an exit door. Its wood framed
with one large, clear pane. I ponder

the delicate nature of a thin plank
of cut pine that holds such thick glass.
I look at the book I am reading. It's about

a young woman who wakes to find
a naked man in her living room. He is wet,
so wet, he seems to leak water. Already

a rug by the fireplace where he lies
is in ruins. This woman, she asks why
is he there, but he doesn't seem to know.

He begs her for water, and when she brings
him a glass, he actually chews the water.
A nurse enters my hall, seven doors left,

only six on the right, because of a shower.
We each get a bath every other day. The nurse
looks left, then right. No one else is awake.

She goes into the room I occupy with another
woman, a dying woman, already past knowing.
Our nurse checks on her, returns to the hall

sending me an empty smile. I return to my book.
Now the woman seems to remember this man,
although he doesn't look entirely human

with his seeping skin and clay-color body.
I'm not at all sure I have the story straight,
nurses, they hand out pain meds and watch

while I take them. These meds make
sentences in my novel run together. I have
to go back and read everything at least twice.

I put my book aside and watch a strange
formation of clouds. Angels, I think,
an immense conclave of angels arranging fate.

# FRONT PORCH SITTING

It has been a brutal summer.
I could almost forget except for
the testimony of parched plants and bushes
scorched by sun.

Even now the sun hides behind tall trees,
backlighting those by the creek path.
There is a coyote den there. Pups announce
their presence during full-moon nights.

My mother walks up the front steps and sits heavily
in an opposing chair as night closes in.
The dead seem to have little to say, so we don't say
much of anything

for not knowing where to start. When everything
is encompassed by the pitch black, I return inside
and leave her sitting there. Morning bears witness
to each crushed cushion.

## ZEN FOR THE LIVING

Wind blows birds right out of the trees.
This is all that is left of a hurricane
as it tore through Galveston, ravaged
Houston, before heading our way.

Newscasters show blown-out windows in high-rises,
papers swept clean from offices. I try not to watch,
dumbfounded with media's choice of offerings.
I've *withdrawn*, you might say.

My preference for news floats on natural air currents:
cicadas' drone, geese flying south, cows in a lower pasture,
autumn's promise in the wind. What grand design—
even God must view TV as miscommunication.

I walk back through the room just as the TV screen
highlights an over-stuffed anchorman standing deep
in swirling water, a microphone crushed to his chest,
a huge wave about to knock him off his feet.

What's that old rhyme, *In place of brains, he thought
God said trains, and he missed his*. This room is
twenty-seven feet long, so I don't have to witness such stupidity
any longer than it takes to turn the TV off.

Later in the morning, I'll sit in church
and beg to be forgiven for a myriad of thoughts.
In the stained glass windows, I'll remind myself,
no one lives who first envisioned this hallowed ground.

## AVALANCHES

What I like best is hugging him,
that moment with my face buried in his neck,

my arms not meeting around him,
his warmth,

then I put things away, start the washer,
feed cats. I make a list,

a list of things that need to be done, clean
everything, everything needs to be cleaned

every day, and lists, I read those lists
between hugs and coffee, order—

bed made, clean bath, clothes put away,
meals, gathering for meals,

lists and bills, mail brings bills
and lists of students, day lists,

night lists, look out the window,
everything orderly, hugs, sleep,

new day of lists. See how light
avalanches through tall windows?

## HASTENING HEADLONG TO A DUSTY END

Only because it's quiet, I hear the hum of our A/C,
then sounds of a train far off. Most times, I do not
hear these everyday sounds.

The sirens I hear, early morning sirens scream,
"Out of our way! Emergency! Lives depend
on our arrival." I concentrate on the breath,

my breath, eyes closed, fully present,
each sound resonates. I release.
Cars rush in the street, I breathe,

an alarm, motorcycle, a dog barks, door slams,
breathe, helicopter overhead. A world in progress,
I breathe, release, and accept, knowing all of us

hasten headlong to a dusty end. Yet the sun
goes down in the west every night, only to rise again,
without any sound at all.

## VALLEY THROUGH THE HILL

Turkey vultures have flown in to sort
through what remains. They turn
and regard my passing vehicle

with territorial fierceness. In my rearview
mirror, I see one seem to hiss as my car
retreats into the roadcut through a hill.

This man-made slice is 340 feet deep
from ridge crest to road level,
an entity of dirt and stone.

It's difficult not to think about the vultures
with my car surrounded by cliffs.
The cut becomes a shroud that hangs over me.

## BETWEEN LIFE AND LOSS
   –for Jillian

A gaggle of geese wings it overhead,
an elm tree's height above me.
Their underbellies are eggs in soft golden light.
Their honking competes with a train whistle,

far off at first, then closer, closer still.
The sun is going down. This October night
brings a chance of rain. You might say
I am planted in this chair.

I'd tie myself in with barbed wire
if it would stop my daughter from leaving
the road. Silence the roaring engine of her car
as it flew across the sky, somersaulted

how many times—I pray to never know.
I must root to this cold ground and wait.
If life was fair, any minute she would appear
with her own daughter who is just now taking

first baby steps. Jillian's arms would be full
of fresh-cut flowers and herbs
from her garden. I can almost hear her
call my name as they swing open

the gate. Maybe I could forgive fate
if today were not so beautiful,
and beautiful too, the day it happened,
and the day after.

# STRING THEORY

Jillian, Jillian, a run-on of sounds pours
through air in a sweet murmur.
I named her that, never willing to leave

well enough alone. Her name had been Jill,
her eyes so blue, everyone who saw them
felt a need to comment.

She had a touch that would heal
a leper. Lovely just to think of her now
without the constant worry

of her straining against every boundary.
I'm sorry for the separation—
who could have predicted ice,

that cliff. And, if I had it to do over,
I might have found a way around
that final argumentative push

that launched the parting of our lives.
It's far too hurtful to think of her life cut short
and so pleasant sitting here this morning

as color spreads across the horizon,
moon still high, and I remember the day she
dyed my eyelashes. How careful she was,

never to lose physical contact. Don't let go
of me now, my darling girl—feel how tightly
I hold that string between our two dimensions.

## THE WATCHER
   –for Willie James King

My birthday is in late June
when a warm Santa Ana
sweeps through the city
and broadleaf ivy spreads
from under the shade of a eucalyptus,
peeks through slats in the whitewashed fence,
bowed from summers of dry desert heat

plus June mornings laden with salty Pacific air.
I find myself watching the gray cottony vastness,
cradling the cat nestled on my chest
as if I live only for these early mornings,
and the hymn of the sea in each long swirl
as it curls toward shore,
the song of wind, stirring in a restless eucalyptus.

The sea wind strokes my face—my bare arms,
as I arc a flat stone to hop across water
and sink into a blue pool bed.
I have learned about solitude—
how to bleed in this balcony and room,
yet lift like smoke in a rainbow's trance.

## FOR THIS, FOR EVERYTHING
## I AM ALMOST OUT OF TIME

I-65 North going into Franklin, I pass a family of buffalo.
The bull positions his hugeness between freeway,

the cow and their calf, the offspring almost as large as his sire.
Just to the right and beyond the buffalo, a white cross stabs

upward in a ditch toward infinity. The name, *John Lunn*,
clearly visible is written on the shoulders of the cross.

I always wave, *Hi, John*, as my car speeds by at 75 mph.
This has been going on for eleven months now, ever since

we arrived in Middle Tennessee. I have caught a speeding
train. It races toward a birthday that is considered by most

rational beings to distinguish old age from middle age.
So plain is it to me that I am moving through these last years

at accelerated speed. It's time I start making contacts,
you understand, who already passed to the other side.

## HOW LONG IS ONE MAN'S TIME ON EARTH?
### HOW LONG MUST THE LIFE OF A WANDERER LAST?
–Tu Fu


A river runs through the Biltmore Estate. It overflowed
its banks on Monday. More rain is predicted by nightfall.

Walking paths disappear into murky waters. Canada
geese ride the river where tall grass rises above the flow.

It's peaceful, serene even. Gray clouds billow above
and quickly change form. The shape of our lives is like this.

We continue to ride the currents. It's possible to be
at the beginning of some grand adventure or at the end.

## GOOD NEWS

News informs us the East is buried in snow.
Temperatures have plunged below zero,

our world has returned to the Ice Age.
Icebreakers plough up the frozen waters
of Boston harbor.

When I was a girl, pain seemed bottomless,
the chill around my heart, a deep crevasse.

But little by little, the sun crept into my life,
warmth spread throughout my days
and I was made whole. Listen—

life endures many changes of temperature.
Every day brings a new sunrise,

every night renews the human spirit.
And take notes here, because night heals,
not all things, but given a chance, it filters—

just look at all the extraordinary light,
how it shines even on a frozen landscape.

## DAYS CONTINUOUS AS STARS THAT SHINE

Pelicans skim the surf's edge, fly past
floating fog. Somewhere nearby, on land,
a mourning dove coos. I am awakened by

my lungs' heaving from congestion.
I dreamt of a safe house on the top floor
of a concrete building where I could sleep,

but only when the body could no longer sustain
itself on catnaps. I'm completely exhausted,
that's my job now: to rest and renew my spirit.

****

The living room has a panoramic view
of the Pacific. It showed me that the surf
is in constant motion. It's so different

from living in a marina. Gulls on open water
are not territorial about air space.
From the wide sea, waves roll toward shore.

My mother was driving home from work—
pulled her car to a curb and died, right there
in the driver's seat, her hands still on

the wheel. I'd like to have her back
now that I'm as old as she was then.
I've grown far more forgiving.

****

The wind came up last night and blew
all the smog and dense fog somewhere else,
but not here, not along the Pacific Coast

where thousands of birds bob on water.
The sea is both dark and restless. Catalina
is visible, I think I can make out buildings

along the shore. Of course, this is ridiculous,
it's twenty-six miles across the channel.
It was never my desire to actually live

by water's edge. I thought that would be
boring really, but it isn't, the sea is always alive—
days have become continuous as stars that shine.

              ****

I wade through these last days here, through
fog that blankets morning's surge. If there are
waves, they slide to shore unnoticed by sky.

There is no wind, no breeze of any kind, no waving
palms, no sand that blows, no spray off combers,
only birds in the tops of trees.

I carry my coffee cup down the steps and out
onto the beach. The air is warm, the sand cools
my feet. The water is truly *as smooth as glass*.

I long for nothing, nothing worth my envy.
Whatever my sorrow, it has been swept out
into the vast, unfettered sea.

## WINTER SONG

Rain returns to puddle around roses,
run off into dry stream beds,
cascade down the sheer face of a cliff.
I can hardly believe this serious wind.

Rain pelts my roof flat.
Cats look up, each eye a yellow candle.
What had I wanted before this season
came to blanket us in wild ambition?

After going to bed last night,
I didn't even try to sleep,
just let pictures unfold in my mind:
carousels of smiling horses—a bear, so soft.

Still, what I wanted was a sparkle of stars overhead,
twins of Gemini rising like their Roman namesakes,
and just south, Sirius at the stern. Even so,
there is this dazzling pattern of broken branches,

a cluster of small fists on the maples.
Perhaps they are bronze pearls, waiting to be strung.
My spirit lifts and strains against our difficult world.
Bring on the driving rain, hail pounding at windows.

When winter is over, spring will rise in the sky,
a feathery bird—all eye and beak,
waiting for morning's first morsel.
There is always the promise of new beginnings.

# SIX
## ABOVE GROUND

*"Oh yet we
trust that
somehow good
will be the
final goal."*

–Alfred,
Lord Tennyson

## OH YET WE TRUST THAT SOMEHOW GOOD
### WILL BE THE FINAL GOAL
–Alfred, Lord Tennyson

Fog hugs the ground, lifts
in immeasurable increments to lace
itself in a canopy of oak trees that
splay their branches across the myriad
creatures below and guards them
as a sacred burden. My father held me so.
He sat with me through long nights
of childhood, and I felt protected.
But his child is no longer a child.
Father has long since become
one with the earth. Each day I belong
more to the soft moist ground myself.
Only the oaks will live on.

# MIDSUMMER'S EVENING WITH RAIN

Waves of lightning streak across the sky.
Heat hangs in the air until tops of trees

droop, wilted. I reach into a bag of potatoes
grown by Amish, still dusted with earth.

Most would use a potato peeler. With three
in a drawer, I choose a paring knife from

the case and slice into the potato's thin
layer of skin. My hands work in circular

movement, maintaining a quarter-inch peel,
steady pressure, a curl of fibrous ribbon that

falls away from its orb of white perfection.
Still, no rain. I cut slices into thin rounds

of flawlessness, then arrange in a small pan.
A slight layer of olive oil, sprinkle sea salt,

dried basil, cut from an herb pot last week.
When it looks like an art project, I fry lightly

until crisp, toss a mixed-green salad, remove
a roasted chicken covered in rosemary from

the oven. Place perfect—dishes, silver, linen,
pour a single crystal goblet of a fine white wine.

Two candelabras grace the table, and to each
I hold a flame. As the last one catches,

a boom of thunder shocks the house silly.
At last, rain falls in sheets, soaking the earth.

# A WALK THROUGH WOODS ON HOOD CANAL

Because I need to feel water's edge,
walk on soggy flats where stones tumble to polish,
I take a rough path down to the canal

and linger only to pick raspberries off the wild vines.
This is solemn labor, each one of us given
just so many days to cherish the crustiness

of our surroundings,
taste sweet burst of continuation.
I carry my own death with me

like an unopened time capsule,
thinking not at all about the chill
lost among trees in morning.

This is no time to grow weary of the green moss
as it spreads or tangles of mistletoe blooming
in witches' brooms. Calm water is just ahead.

This is living, knowing the strength which comes
from a centered place and is instinctive as breath
flow in, then out. This is about letting go of fear.

# FLIGHT

You know the path that runs along the creek in Topanga—
follow it long enough and it spills into the Pacific Ocean.
I was dreaming I had walked that old path
when the sound of splashing awakened me.

I lay there wandering between two worlds: sleep and dawn,
until such thrashing —it became impossible.
Dogs—in the spa—two black labs
cavorting, tongues lolling,

and I swear, they were smiling,
positively frivolous with joy.
Their names were Rough and Tough,
according to their collars,

and when I called the number on their tags,
their owner came for them.
Even their departure was cause for great jubilation.
Today, years later, I sit on a beach

watching two women, well into their sixties,
walking along the water's edge,
fully clothed, carrying large flowered umbrellas
of clashing colors.
I think about that path the dogs ran

through the long night, and how these women too,
look as if they have walked the shifting sands
for years maybe, so driven are we all.
A shadow in the shape of a bird traverses the sand.

I would collapse if I weren't already seated
by the duality of place and flight—
life at its relentless pace
and as close as I get to prayer,

I address the gods of departure,
remind them to guard the seven portals of this world.
I'm not ready to leave yet. Even now the moon
crosses the sky on a million-mile journey.

# TROUBLED ASPECT TO AN ECLIPSED MOON IN LEO

I wake thinking about death. There is so little
time left, twenty years, if I'm lucky—

so little time, such a long time,
yet both are true, according to the Tao.

I stay in bed and close my eyes once more.
I open my eyes again, and it is quiet.

From across the road a cow disrupts
the low ground fog with her breath.

The Canada geese call in response.
Then that great body of geese rises as one.

In the air they form the long vee shape
that will take them to another pasture,

another pond, another time. My head
is heavy, my body feels waterlogged

and weighted. I am drowning in the sea
of what will become my last years.

## LIST OF DECEASED

It arrived as an attachment,
so I downloaded, knowing full well

it would upset me. I would not have believed
a whole page, each name centered,

spaced one to a line, top to bottom.
I didn't have the nerve to count them.

I thought, *Maybe it's good there isn't room
for even one more name on this sheet.*

But my rational mind said, *A second sheet
could be started.* No, this was unthinkable.

So I read from the top, read each name
of my tribe, the ones I went to high school with,

each seventeen-year-old face still imprinted
in my mind's eye as if it is just another Friday,

with school starting at 8 AM, and out at 3 PM,
after the weekend, we'll do it all over again.

# TRAVELING AT NIGHT

When I think of my daughter returning
after what would be a short death,

I think of her feeding animals, pitchforks
full of fresh hay to horses, seed to the birds,

a plate full of Spring Mix to wild bunnies.
No, that was me feeding Spring Mix to bunnies.

The last time I saw my girl on this plane, she walked
through a doorway of an Indian restaurant

where we had agreed to meet. Scarves draping
the walls painted brunt red that accented her white

linen suit, red that picked up highlights
woven into her long dark hair as it fell

over her shoulders. Those astonishing china-blue
eyes searched the room for me. Already,

she seemed to see past infinity. Can you understand
my waking in the middle of night to find the room

filled with grief so that getting up and turning
all the lights on made sense, then turning them off

again, so I could pretend well into light
of morning, I too, had already gone to the next plane.

## AFTER A LONG WAR

I thought I had done something, perhaps
something wrong, something that hurt
my father as I'd danced around

a fountain, chased the many
colored lights, wondering if
the water itself was different colors.

At five, I already knew things were
often not what they seemed, so I sat
beside him without swinging my feet

or snatching at droplets of color
or singing the strange song
that interrupted my thoughts

as my father's shoulders shook
and his tears fell in a furious storm.
It was his first afternoon back,

back from war. My mother sent us out,
get to know each other, she had said.
Me, the singer of senseless melodies.

He, caught in what would be a lifetime
of survivor's guilt. Something no five-year-old
should ever get to know.

## FISHING

The summer I was twenty,
Father was sober.

We fished off the pier.
I wanted him to bait my hook.

He said, *Kid,*
*learn to do it yourself.*
*Life gets messy.*

After summer is over,
after he starts drinking again,

*Marry young, Kid,* he says,
*blondes fade fast.*

# FISHING FOR ANSWERS

*He lives*, the psychic says, *just talk to him*,
she means that I am not to assume my father
can't hear me. He tells her to remind me that
*I'm nobody's baby but his*, and he kisses her

on the cheek. *I can feel it*, she says,
this woman wearing a yellow flowered sundress
and bright orange lipstick. She makes conversing
with the dead seem normal. So now, fifty years later

my father has moved past the terrible hospital.
He is no longer hooked up to machines, no longer
flails his arms in pain, begging for mercy.

That was back then, now he's kissing the cheek
of a pretty psychic telling her that I'm his baby.
His baby, he doesn't see how old I've grown,
how much older I am than himself before he died.

That father doesn't remember screaming my name,
a scream that wakes me even today
where I plead for help to an empty room
that is hospital white and no one answers.

# SNOW BEFORE NOON

So much fall in the air! Pop-up roses
still flourish, and there is the gift

of a second bloom of irises. Our cats
are tired from sitting at an open window

last night listening to coyotes howl before
a skunk made its way through the yard.

Church services are at the Conway farm,
10 AM, and then potluck to follow.

I make a chicken salad. Put the heavy
dish in the freezer so everything will

stay cold while we pray—and I need
to pray. I need help. No, that isn't

exactly right, what I need is my spirit
lifted. I have friends who are sick, and one

has just lost her husband. She could use
my prayers—children and grandchildren,

so many need help, and I do pray—
I pray for their comfort, for peace, for

restoration. I pray for myself, for more soul,
for health and, as temperatures plunge

and snow flurries swirl in the air, I pray
for a sudden breath of sweet youth.

# LOVE NEEDS TO BE SET ALIGHT AGAIN AND AGAIN
—William Matthews

After the final rinse of hot water,
she reaches for a towel. Then begins
a ritual of the squeegee: first the glass,

then shower's tiled sides, the floor.
What's left of the water she'll dry
with a clean cloth, snowy white, until

it is damp and moist enough
to give a soft shine to the bathroom sinks
and counters. She stands naked before

a mirror wondering, if her heart
stopped now, and this, this ordinary task,
completed her life, who would care?

On her knees, sorting through an old filing cabinet,
she tosses more than is kept.
She finds a folder stuffed with greeting cards,

years of birthday wishes, notes on all subjects
and what appears to be a vintage
Christmas card. She admires the elaborate

wreath, its satin ribbon threaded through
small slits in painted boughs.
What on earth, she mutters, opening the card.

In her father's hand, recognizable by its bold,
straight style, distinct as cursive, and printed
some fifty years before:

*You'll always be my baby, don't forget—DAD.*

## A NEW HEART IN HEAVEN

I look forward to winter solstice
and the shortest day of the year.
In honor of this, I write out

all my disappointments, my losses
and grief from the year past and burn them
in a pagan fire. Yet I find I don't want to let go—

grief is all that's left after my daughter's
car flew her from the highway into the afterlife.
I try to remember the smell of her skin,

instead I see the heart she once drew and colored
pink and purple, with yellow stars at the center.
She was five then, and this heart loomed as wide

as her bedroom wall. I imagine it now, pulsating,
yellow stars swimming to the edges of her world
before vaulting beyond, into the next.

## TO THE LIVING

Each day this frozen landscape is the same—yet different,
the direction wind blows off the Pachaug River, the way
trees cycle from barren, as they are now, toward green
and wild. A graveyard sits high on a plateau
across the river, then narrows at the back end

of my brother's property. Generations of Normans
and Greers lie under a mist of time; chiseled stones
are worn smooth from centuries of New England winters.
In spring, my brother's dog and I cross the bridge
to fields where hay and corn were cut months earlier

to lay in for cold weather. Down rows of headstones,
we work our way across to the farthest end
where markers long forgotten lie flat in weeds.
With his nose, the dog pushes brown growth away
from a fallen stone, exposing barely visible script.

By turning this way and that, catching different angles of light,
I make out a name, Cassie Ann, and her age, which was two,
and the year, so long past, grief must have taken them all.
We press on—zig to the right, around a bordering stone fence,
then to left, past a Christmas tree farm. Finally we see

the back of my brother's place, the porch he just built,
white siding, his seven-year-old dancing in the yard,
a picture of celebration. The dog runs ahead, ears back
and flopping in the breeze. All of us—just happy
to be above ground, grateful for each blessed day.

## AND THE PROCESS GOES ON

We own this space and have lived here for the past five years,
but each day I pour though pictures of listings in another place,
a different city, and ask questions only I can answer. This one

perhaps, that one, or maybe next week a listing will appear
that might be perfect, if I just wait. I don't like carpet, and
this new space, in another city, must have trees and a deck

to enjoy trees. Nine-foot ceilings tend to crush my spirits, so light,
yes, light is important. Funny how I spent the first half, no,
more than half, maybe two-thirds, who can count

unless maybe a psychic has knowledge, but then it seems
far-fetched. I collected gold, to be sure, and silver too, crystal,
fine china, oils and watercolors. I simply love watercolors.

Then as life would have it, I paired up and pared down.
For years, I've eliminated, tossed, given away, detached
until, until, more needs to be done.

Each leaving, another door to walk though, another, another—
and where am I now? Old by many standards, still walking
through doors, still walking. And the process goes on.

# EVEN ABOVE GROUND

Winter closes in, putting an end
to autumn. The sun slinks further
and further south. The time comes

when I realize whole days have passed
without my hearing a single Canada goose.
The flame bushes that yesterday crowded

my landscape with fiery color
are now just part of soft browns,
meek wards of the Earth.

Frost whitens every blade of grass. Trees
stand naked and quivering. Night steals in
early, while light blinds all the windows

in a scattering of houses. From thousands
of chimneys, smoke escapes. Our cats spend
entire afternoons in their heated lamb's-wool beds

while I negotiate my final instructions—
sign, date, notarize *and being of sound
mind, this, my last will and testament.*

## PRAYERS FOR OLIVER

Spring rain—I kneel in tall grass as
dogwood petals drift pale across

our lawn. The dainty layers, wafer thin,
brush my bare arms. If I were to lay one

on my tongue in communion, what then?
Already the downy woodpeckers trust

my offering of seed—finches chant,
cardinals build for future generations.

Today news came of death, a new soul
born dying. For his journey, a new moon

will rise and that means continuation. A new
summer will reign in sixty days.

For we who remain, another lesson in letting go.
We are all returned to become one with earth.

For now, we speak a language of grief,
its brokenhearted cry has become a wail.

# FEBRUARY'S FLOWERS

To see just how far I'd come,
I took a pillow from the other side of the bed
and put it behind my back.
This was my husband's pillow,
the one that cradled his head.
I'd thought about cushioning my back
from the hard wood of the headboard
but hadn't wanted to claim
that side of the bed.
I'm careful at night too,
never to stray from my own flowered side.
Now my feet—
that's a different story,
it seems they have a mind of their own.
They search, wake me with their cold findings.

Winter has come.
I fling a heavy quilt over the bed.
Now when I slide between the flowered sheets,
my head drunk with fatigue,
I sleep—sleep and dream:
roses bursting forth with dazzling fragrance,
pink azaleas with ten thousand separate blooms,
green blades of grass trembling toward the sun,
and yellow buttercups dusting the air—
the Earth radiant, and me,
surprised to find myself still alive.

## ON A STREET NAMED HAZELTON

Home was west of downtown Los Angeles,
row after row of rough stucco buildings
duplicated cookie-cutter faithful
on a street named Hazelton.

That name was a synonym for poverty,
with its crumbling walls, bushes,
crouched like muggers, low to the ground.
After I left home, I moved north to Calabasas.

My best friend, Jean,
she headed south to La Habra,
and I'm not positive about this,
but I don't think either of our mothers

ever set foot in a house
as grand as what we both live in now.
I drove back there the other day.
Hazelton has a new name; the old one got

a bad reputation. The clotheslines were gone,
so were the open fields where we played.
More miserable buildings have been planted
in those fields.

The fences, sidewalks, and stucco
are scarred with names like Stubby, Speedy, and Sly.
The asphalt street doesn't feel like home anymore.
I wanted to return one last time

and capture for just a frozen moment
the toothy laughter of youth and remember
where it all started before being forced
to understanding, how it all ends.

## SAYING THE UNSAYABLE

A new class today, five students, their cheery smiles
turn to tears within minutes. First, the woman
whose husband died a few months before,
then a man, his wife of sixty-two years,

dead six weeks. Another woman starts to tell us
about going with a group to help Haitians
after an earthquake. Dry eyed
until today, a dam of tears breaks.

I watch two other students; I know one
lost her mother recently and grief is just below
the surface. The other woman has that guarded
look of a dog just brought home from a shelter,

a dog not sure it can trust anyone. She's there
in the room but near a door, checking to make sure
it's still unlocked, and me, wondering if I can lead
another class through a process of saying the unsayable.

After I return home, I check the mail, the usual bills,
*The New Yorker* still hasn't figured out I already subscribe
and encourages me to take advantage of their generous
offer. There's an envelope from my daughter's husband,

pictures of their child, this child growing up motherless,
nine years old, six years since my daughter died—
for six years I've showed up to the page and still
haven't found any way to say the unsayable.

## ONE WORD

Wind had blown up a gale and it rained
all night, but the occasion eludes me now.

It might have been anything, a birthday, graduation,
somebody's wedding, it was that long ago.

Our skins had turned sepia on paper.
Mother stands pretty as any cherished wife.

Dad walks in from his other life
just long enough to take his rightful place.

My brother is smiling from ear to ear,
but I remember Mom giving him a slap

and now that I look closer, I see it's not a smile
but a grimace, falling onto the rigid shoulders

of a small boy with a crew cut. I stand apart,
leaving a hole between me and my family

large enough for a bicycle to pass. Wishing too,
the hole larger still, like a continent maybe.

And if I know anything, there is emptiness,
too spent for anger, yet I'm smiling too.

I might have survived that day better if there had
been a word, one word to sum it all up,

but the right word didn't come along for years,
*dysfunctional*, we were a dysfunctional family.

## THE LONG YEAR OF YOUTH

Only once I dressed as a boy,
golden hair slicked back with Brylcreem,
borrowed white shirt, blue tie, black slacks,

bone thin, so I could still pull off that look.
No need to bind the promise of breasts
at thirteen. All this for an elective.

My part was to play the "pop" in "Pop Goes
the Weasel," so unaccomplished, yet
made to feel pride at the importance in my role

by Mr. Emile Schillio, our junior high school
teacher. How could I guess he would be the one
for whom I would set my own standards,

this fresh-faced, round man smelling of
saddle soap and starch, who shed real tears
when my mother asked about my talent

for the violin. His head bowed, as in grief,
while my instrument sighed in its case, he said,
"Sewing might be a more successful class."

## THE BARRISTER'S BEDROOM

We called him "The Barrister" as he slipped
between two doorways of what became his life.

Light always burned so that even in the darkest part
of night, we never knew which room he occupied.

Either asleep or reading, both rooms were filled
with books on every subject, leather bound,

first editions, signed with admiration.
We called him Grandfather, but when we spoke of him,

it was always, "The Barrister." Mother would say,
"Go ask The Barrister" with our million questions.

And he did know everything, I swear,
I never asked a question he couldn't answer.

He always made us feel smart for asking,
inviting us in one at a time for what he called a "chat."

After I went away to school, and before I returned,
he was gone, but those two rooms remained as they were.

Tonight, still in need of counsel before the wrecking ball,
I've ended up here, where the scent of wild lemon

that was his aftershave remains tangible.
Even now in these the darkest of hours.

# READING THE STARS

## I

My brother tells me about his trip to Belize,
rainforest and hiking to a river,
wide and swift. There, he saw a rope

and knew, just like we all know when a time
comes for some action extraordinary,
he must cross that river of fury,

Tarzan-like. He considered how lucky
he was—how many of us never
see the rope that saves us.

## II

My young student, youngest
I've ever worked with, is writing
what she calls a "period piece,"

1990's, she says, and here I was
thinking how 1990 seems
like yesterday, right?

## III

My temples throb, my right foot hurts,
sharp pains play ring around the rosie
in my ribcage. Twenty pounds of cat jumps in my lap.

My notebook is propped on the cat's back,
my pen makes its way across the page,
the cat purrs, occasionally makes a star foot.

## IV

My husband tells me that Jupiter is in my fifth house,
which means I'd better write my ass off or Jupiter's
energy will be enacted in ways I won't like.

V

Reading John Bennett's work for a couple weeks now,
a "wild man" only because he writes it like it is.
I got a submission from John when I was an editor

all those years back. I've read everything the man
has ever written. That's something John
and I share, our lives on paper.

My cat jumps down and I'm covered in fur.
I had fresh clothes on just an hour ago.
The pain in my ribcage is gone like the pounding

in my head. I'll have to walk to see how the foot is.
Jupiter seems appeased for the present.
My brother arrives Monday with his wife.

John Bennett is still in the great Northwest
washing windows and writing every day.
I'm here, in the South. This is what we do, write!

# RITUALS

I must have read this someplace,
or maybe someone told me,
but radishes will grow before a man
can starve to death.
Imagine—nothing to eat for days,
then holding a solitary radish,
red, a root.
It might be divided in half,
then placed on the tip of a tongue.
Just think, the cool heat of it.

I remember a myriad of rituals
for survival,
like the ceremony of making money,
and it's true that I've lived
in a house of discontent.
I've seen the arc of a shooting star.
I know just how cold the moon is.

I've witnessed the complexity
of melting commitments,
mystical communion
of ultimate realities.
It's all a dull ache
spreading across my shoulders.

My stomach is full of rocks.
There is the sand of five wars in me.
I am up to my armpits in swamp water.
Today is my fifty-third birthday.
I say these things so that you will know:
Do not put your faith in me.
I haven't gathered a single seed
to plant radishes.

# END OF SEASON

It was almost February, for heaven's sake,
before she took Christmas lights down.
The wreath with red-glazed bulbs
and spruce branches would have to go.

Before she knew it, spring would amble
up the street wearing a touch of green.
Then she could watch birds steal raffia
from around a different wreath.

She was all for nest building, but with
each new spring, she grew more concerned.
It would be one year less to get her nest
finished. She isn't able to say why,

but she remembered traveling and how she tossed
her keys into a suitcase. Returning home,
she found them missing from among her things.
It was late, too late to call anyone for help,

so she picked up a good-sized rock and broke
a window. After knocking all the glass aside,
she crawled into her own home, humbled
by such a thing. Her nest now had broken shards

of glass to sweep away. Make no mistake,
seasons *are* adding up. All the rocks in the garden
wouldn't change the facts. Her mind was still clear,
even if her knees were a tad stiff.

Every day is like the one before. She considers
time to be like that window, just waiting to splinter.
Everything shatters eventually,
and there is always someone left sweeping.

## AFTERGLOW

My right elbow hurts. Last week
it was my left thumb or maybe my knee.
It hasn't always been like this.
Just a short time ago
I leapt from my morning bed,
made it quick to seal in warmth,
ran mostly naked in some lace thing
just long enough to cover the bare.

I didn't even own a robe. Back then,
diamond stars ran up the heels of my shoes.
Now, it's this elbow, my thumb,
these knees, singing their own odd song.
Passing by a store window, I see
an exquisite French lace slip, champagne
color and costing a fortune. I purchase
it anyway, bring it home and wear it to bed.

There is a sound lace makes moving
through air, cooling in flight, lingering
a little before it comes to rest
on the bedroom floor. Hearing that sound
brought everything back, all of it,
leaping, being *that* young, *that* pretty,
*that* desired.

## OLD AGE

A warm breeze drifts though our bedroom window,
explores the sleeping cats. Lamps allow their shades

to tremble, ceiling gathers what it can: dreams,
dust, the bark of a dog far off and across a pasture.

I would bark, but it seems unseemly for a woman
my age. There is a full moon in Pisces. I saw hawk

circling our field to the south earlier. He was hunting
for some unfortunate who looked for a new beginning.

## SUNDAY
–for Justin and Erik

Two boys came through my house
today. Two, wild-with-life buddies,
curving their young bodies into furniture

only to wrestle free an instant later,
handling things they had never seen
with their many fingers.

They went about whispering and prodding,
happiest when they could move
through a passageway to all outdoors.

Writing arguments on nothing more
than pure energy. Two small boys, sharing
their years and size but from different seeds

of restlessness, speaking in code
only they understood, even then not all the time.
I'm telling you, something moved through me

slicing my heart open seeing them go.
It wasn't about their going—
it was the way their heads were bent,

busy with seat belts. And the way
they raised their arms to wave at the same time.
Or maybe their grins, so pleased about things.

A siren went by at the precise moment
they disappeared from view, the piercing sound
warbling in my heart, now half a century old.

# FROM THE PORCH RAILING

The sun has risen to top the hill behind
our property, risen as quickly as
the new school just built. Bright rays

of sunlight shine through open windows,
through double-wide doors of welcome,
so that it has the look of a giant jack-o'-lantern,

although it's only May. By end of October,
the plan is for all our rambunctious
school-aged minds to gather and celebrate

a ritual of higher learning. But for today,
light is what fills the doors, spills through
windows, while school halls remain quiet.

## BECAUSE IT'S DARK

Sometimes I hear the front door open,
close. This happens at night, house
dark, kittens asleep, my husband

warm beside me, and I would swear
I am awake. I don't bother getting up,
not anymore. No, I never see anything

out of the ordinary. My wandering
just wakes the cats, adds to their confusion:
Morning? Not morning? Morning?

When my daughter was very young,
she would wake screaming at night.
Of course, I would run to her. Once,

I asked why she screamed and she said,
"Because it's dark." I told her stars bring us
the only light at night so we can sleep.

"Oh," she said, and that was the last time
she ever woke screaming. I've thought about
a chair under the doorknob to end

any open and closing business, but then
too, could it be my daughter, or my father?
What if the dead come to me at night,

knowing that I'm awake, waiting?

## LIVE ENOUGH OF WHAT YOU'VE ALWAYS DREAMED AND THERE'S NO ROOM LEFT FOR FEELING BAD
–Richard Bach

5 AM, cats fed! Already, they have returned to bed.
Birds not yet up, their bent legs locked into sleep,

resting their birdie brains in readiness so they can
spread their wings and ride the wind. Thin light comes

from an eastern horizon as I toss raw peanuts
on the ground for our resident chipmunk.

Morning set, soon to bloom forth. These random acts
of kindness done with steady hands no longer young,

yet not so old that I can't revel at the prospect of hundreds
of such mornings, still in the making.

# THE MORNING PORCH

A red sun creeps around the bottom of a silo,
then struggles to be free of barn and cows.

Given time, the light will lord it over pastureland,
mares and foals, a creek that empties into a pond.

That sun will rise, rise in the heavens
until it starts its descent to the far side of the world.

Robins have claimed an area around a dogwood
and have built a wonder of construction intricately

woven at the bottom of a tree's foliage.
Robins of the South are good-sized birds.

That nest, area surrounding, even leaves, they have laid
claim to as surely as if it had been surveyed,

given a lot and tract number, recorded and taxed.
The birds allow me on the porch. Our cows moo,

our horses graze, a fat sun falls behind the hill
and leaves it all to the fireflies that light the grounds

at nightfall. Each morning I beg for all this again
so that I might swim into the abyss of such pleasure,

bathe in it again and again and again,
a glutton at this age in my life.

**STELLASUE LEE** was a founding editor at *RATTLE*, a poetry journal, and is now editor *Emerita*. She is a host of WordStream on WDVX, Knoxville, TN with Linda Parsons. Two of her books have been entrants for the Pulitzer Prize, *Firecracker Red*, and *Crossing The Double Yellow Line*. She is the winner of the grand prize in Poetry To Aide 2013 by Humanity Al Falah in Malaysia. Dr. Lee received her Ph.D. from Honolulu University.

Made in the USA
Columbia, SC
16 February 2022

56338270R00152